PEOPLE POWER

Grass Roots Politics and Race Relations

Judith N. DeSena

University Press of America,® Inc.
Lanham • New York • Oxford

Copyright © 1999 by
University Press of America,® Inc .
4720 Boston Way
Lanham, Maryland 20706

12 Hid's Copse Rd.
Cumnor Hill, Oxford OX2 9JJ

Library of Congress Cataloging-in-Publication Data

DeSena, Judith N.
People power : grass roots politics and race relations / Judith N. DeSena.
p.   cm.
Includes bibliographical references and index.
1. Community organization—New York (State)—New York Case studies. 2. Women in community organization—New York (State)—New York Case studies. 3. Citizens' associations—New York (State)—New York Case studies. 4. Neighborhood—New York (State)—New York Case studies. 5. Brooklyn (New York, N.Y.)—Politics and government. I. Title.
HN80.N5D42   1999   307.3'362'097471—dc21   99—32759 CIP

ISBN 0-7618-1461-2 (cloth: alk. ppr.)
ISBN 0-7618-1462-0 (pbk: alk. ppr.)

This book is dedicated to my husband Neil, with whom I share this common history, to my son Francis, a future activist, and in memory of those Coalition members who have passed on.

Contents

ACKNOWLEDGEMENTS

There are many people responsible for assisting me in carrying out this study and completing this book. I would like to take this opportunity to express my appreciation.

Gerald Taylor was influential in arranging the acquisition of reports filed by the Greenpoint-Williamsburg Coalition of Community Organizations with the Campaign for Human Development. Gabriella Starita actually copied and obtained those reports for me. Joel Gallob entrusted me with his morgue of local newspapers. Without these data, this analysis would not be possible. I am most grateful to them.

Christine Gargan Casiano transcribed hours of tape recorded interviews, and Laura Starita edited the manuscript for clarity of expression. I am sincerely thankful for their work. I am especially indebted to Meredyth Otlin who spent countless hours assisting me in numerous revisions of the manuscript, and Gabriela Cosma helped prepare it for publication.

St. John's University supported this work by granting me a reduced teaching schedule. I am particularly grateful to Sister Margaret John Kelly, D.C., Reverend David O'Connell C.M. and Dr. Willard Gingerich for encouraging my work.

My husband, Neil Sheehan, is actually co-author. This book, in some ways, documents our love story. Its publication would not have been possible without his insights and ideas, his ability to challenge my thinking, and his willingness to spend endless hours discussing this project, reading each chapter, and suggesting revisions. Most importantly, throughout each phase of the research and writing, he was able to love me unconditionally. I dedicate this book to him. I am thankful to my son, Francis, for serving as a constant reminder that there is more to life than work.

My friends and colleagues critically evaluated my analysis at various stages of the study. Those who come to mind are: Jerome Krase, Angela Danzi, Jeffrey Kraus, Bill DiFazio, Terry Haywoode, Celene Krauss, Lorraine Cohen, Viola Lechner, Helen Sheehan, and Dawn Esposito. I appreciate their remarks. Finally, I am indebted to the participants of the Greenpoint-Williamsburg Coalition of Community Organizations.

PREFACE

This book is a study of a community coalition in northern Brooklyn, which held traditional authority accountable for maintaining municipal services and implementing neighborhood improvements. The Coalition used a confrontational style of organizing. The analysis has three major themes: community power, positive race and ethnic relations, and women's local activism. The approach of this book is interdisciplinary.

Discussions on power in the social sciences focus on elites as the ruling class and major decision makers. The same theme pervades the literature on community power. This book critically evaluates the social science literature on how ordinary people exercise power and offers community activism as an addition. Thus, People Power investigates the potential of community organizations in the politicization of working class and poor people. It argues that participation in community organizations can empower residents to challenge government and corporations, and attempt to influence the outcome of policy decisions regarding municipal services, and the future of neighborhoods. In addition, this study contends that those who are empowered through community organizations are transformed politically, particularly in the areas of political participation, sustained civic involvement, and racial attitudes.

Analyses on urban neighborhoods have given little attention to community cooperation and organization among people with diverse cultural roots. The focus of most studies has been on competition and conflict among various ethnic and racial groups who reside in urban neighborhoods (DeSena 1990; Kornblum 1974; Krase 1982; Molotch 1972; Rieder 1985; Susser 1982; Suttles 1968). The conflict and competition, for the most part, has been over "turf" and other limited resources, such as housing, jobs, and municipal services. People Power illustrates the potential of community organizations in fostering community co-operation and social unity among various ethnic and racial groups. In the course of "doing power," this community coalition recruited residents of diverse races and ethnic groups who worked together effectively on neighborhood issues. Residents set aside apprehensions and tensions stemming from their cultural differences for the sake of the community's needs. This study demonstrates that community organizations have the ability to challenge participants' stereotypical perceptions of race and ethnicity as well as raise their political consciousness. This investigation reveals community co-operation and suggests a model for dealing with conflicts stemming from cultural diversity and racism in urban locales.

Also included is an examination of women's activism, an often neglected area of inquiry in urban studies. This study shows how women are the "rank and file" of community work. On an informal level, women appear to be engaged in idle chatter as they escort their children to and from school, gather in playgrounds, and commute to and from work. A closer investigation reveals that behavior which appears to be "gossip" is actually the creation and maintenance of social networks in which information about the community is passed. Local women educate residents about community issues and mobilize them for meetings and protests. Women were in the forefront of leadership as members of the Coalition. They led rallies and confronted politicians. They were not passive or accepting of neighborhood problems.

The issue of citizen participation is also reasoned and addressed in the manuscript. People Power indicates that through community organizations like the Coalition, ordinary people partake in the democratic process. The Coalition serves as a model of participatory democracy on a local level. Moreover, multi-ethnic unity and politicization evolved from the process of community struggle.

CHAPTER 1

INTRODUCTION

Discourses on power in the social sciences typically focus on a political economy which involves corporate and government elites (Domhoff 1979; Dye 1976; Fitch 1993; Mills 1956). The interactions between corporations and government create interlocking directorates in which CEOs also occupy positions on boards of directors and trustees of universities, hospitals, foundations, and other not for profit groups. In these varied roles, elites make investment and policy decisions which effect the lives of ordinary people. Even discussions on community power assume that local elites are in charge (Lynd and Lynd 1929; Hunter 1953; Vidich and Bensman 1968; Lichten 1986; Fitch 1993). These analyses carry class, race, and gender biases. Ordinary people exercise power in ways which are different from elites. One way, which is the focus of this book, is through community activism.

This book focuses on the empowerment and politicization of ordinary people through community activism, and examines community activism as political behavior. It analyzes the potential of community organizations in the politicization of working class and poor people. This study indicates that a function of community organizations is to socialize ordinary people about politics in the same way that family, schools, and work assume the task. Community organizations educate people about politics. Community organizations channel the energy of ordinary people into political action which may lead to an interest and greater involvement in electoral politics. Participation in community organizations empowers residents to direct and challenge government and corporations, and thus, influence the outcome of policy decisions regarding municipal services and the future of neighborhoods. This study contends that those who are empowered through community organizations are transformed, particularly in the areas of political participation, sustained civic involvement, and racial attitudes.

The movement for "community control" in the 1960's was an assertion about the need for participatory democracy in which ordinary people could devise and implement social policy. It was a movement which focused on "government by the people." Citizens declared "... that key positions should be filled through election; that the ultimate source of agency sovereignty rests in its clients and should be expressed through community control" (Fainstein and Fainstein 1974, 8). Community control functions as a form of political participation on a local level, and can serve as an agent of social change and also defuse tensions among various groups. The legacies of the community control movement currently take the form of citizens' organization's such as the Association of Community Organizations for Reform Now (ACORN), Citizen Action, and the Industrial Areas Foundation (IAF), as well as local planning groups, such as school boards and community boards. These latter planning committees, at present, are comprised of local elites and representatives of special interest groups, a composition which undermines the very intention of community control and, thus, supports the elite model of community power. Evidence exists of both the continued need and opportunity for community control in American cities and towns. The riots in Crown Heights, Brooklyn in 1991 and South Central Los Angeles in 1992 are prime examples of what can happen when people are blocked from and neglected by the decision making process (Salak 1993; Delk 1995). The events leading to these riots serve as the catalysts for expressing anger stemming from oppression. In contrast, the mobilization and co-operation of local leaders, residents, institutions, and government created the Nehemiah Plan in 1981 (Ross 1995), which financed and built low-income housing in poor, African-American communities in Brooklyn.

This book focuses on the demand for and practice of participatory democracy by an activist community coalition, and examines local empowerment and race and ethnic relations through political participation. Multi-ethnic unity and politicization evolved from the process of community struggle. Despite well-established social science literature which focuses primarily on electoral politics, I contend that everyday community activism constitutes political behavior. Within this context is the possibility for community co-operation and racial and ethnic harmony among people of diverse cultural backgrounds. Another major focus of this study is the political participation of low income women through their involvement in grass roots collective struggles.

Ordinary people exercise power through political participation. For the most part, political participation has been conceptualized in limited ways. A review of the literature on political behavior must begin with the basic question, How does one come to participate in politics and, therefore, become political? Political behavior is learned in a variety of ways, specifically through social institutions such as family, peer group, school, and work place. Often, these institutions direct individuals toward the electoral process as the primary venue for political involvement (Lea 1982; Harrigan 1993). For example, schools offer classes in civics which present the role of the citizenry in governance. Children raised in families in which members engage in and discuss politics, may be influenced by the family's viewpoint to undertake political activity. In addition, friends and other menbers of informed networks can influence the politics of others. The institution of work,has also been analyzed noting that unlike their European counterparts, U.S. workers have not united politically to form their own political party (Hocking and Husbands 1976; Huizinga 1972; Katznelson 1982). A number of studies identify the working class in the United States as lacking class consciousness and political unity (Kornblum 1974; Katznelson 1982; Susser 1982; 1988). The creation of a political party which would have an impact on the electoral process is central to discussions of political participation. Most researchers on political participation see the development of a political party as necessary to affect the electoral process. However, there are those analyses which take exception with this view of the working class and contend that they are conscious of their class position (Jackman and Jackman 1983; Wright 1985; Vanneman and Cannon 1987; Fantasia 1988). This viewpoint argues that the actions of the working class must be studied instead of focusing on their opinions (Morris 1992, 356). Furthermore, even though American labor has not created its own political party, "the course of organized labor has been profoundly political" (Aronowitz 1983, xiv) because of the struggle for better working conditions.

Classic models of political participation include voting, campaigning, using citizens' organizations, and contacting an elected official (Verba and Nie 1972). For the most part, the literature has emphasized electoral participation over other types (Verba and Nie 1972; Kleppner 1982; Lea 1982). A tradition in the social sciences has been to examine voting behavior, voter turn-out, and voting trends as indicators of political behavior (Campbell, Converse, and Miller 1960; Nie, Verba, and Petrocik 1976; Wolfinger and Rosenstone 1980; Teixeira 1992). Voting has been viewed as the major way in which citizens exert the greatest pressure on public officials, while the other forms of participation serve to inform politicians of voters' preferences (Verba and Nie 1972; Kleppner 1982). "Voting pressure makes leaders more sensitive to the informative messages conveyed by citizens through other modes of participation" (Kleppner 1982, 6).

Despite the importance placed on voting, voter turn-out continues to decline on a regular basis with few exceptions (Kleppner 1982; Shienbaum 1984). In 1896, 85 percent of eligible voters cast their ballots. By 1960, 65 percent of the electorate voted and this number diminished to 55 percent in 1992 (Squire et. al. 1995, 159). In the 1996 Presidential election, 49 percent of eligible voters turned out (Schmitt 1996). In examining segments of the nation it is noted

> ...the recent trends in turnout evidenced by the nation's 32 largest metropolitan areas deserve some special comment... The center cities begin a sharp decline in 1948; the suburbs begin a more moderate decline in 1944. These long-term secular shifts are of considerable importance because 1) these metropolitan areas constitute over 40% of the national electorate; and 2) the cities and suburbs that compose them are highly partisan. Since 1932 the center cities have returned the largest Democratic margins of victory...their suburbs have been among the most Republican of these locales since the turn of the century. Because of their size and partisan allegiances, these cities and suburbs have been the key to statewide elections in their respective states (Nardulli, Dalager, Greco 1996, 489).

Television news analyses of low rates of voting contend that the American electorate is apathetic. However, there are other factors to consider. For example, low turn-out may be the result of people believing that there is no contest among candidates in some races rather than disinterest, and pre-election polling can effect turn-out. The decline in voting is especially notable among those who are poorly educated and have low incomes.

> Persistently low turnout among working class citizens relieves elected officeholders of even the likelihood of a retrospective electoral sanction...Since it is disproportionately

> working class citizens who "don't count," in this sense, their
> economic interests continue to remain outside the political
> agenda. They play no role in shaping the solutions, because
> they have become irrelevant to defining the problems"
> (Kleppner 1982, 162).

However, there are some exceptions to this. In the 1996 election, Hispanics voted in record numbers (Ayres 1996) and voiced their concern about changes in welfare and immigration laws. Conversely, educated and affluent citizens do vote regularly, and therefore, their issues dominate the political agenda.

Ordinary people also participate politically through social movements. Profound social changes have occurred in American society because of social movements. Social scientists have documented, critically analyzed and evaluated the labor movement (Bernstein 1970; 1971), civil rights (Morris 1984) and welfare rights movements (Piven and Cloward 1977), community control of schools (Berube and Gittell 1969; Fainstein and Fainstein 1974), the women's movement (Echols 1989; Freeman 1975) and the neighborhood movement (Boyte 1980; 1984). Yet, theorists disagree on the effects of collective action. Some argue that these efforts usually fail (Tilly 1978; Katznelson 1982; Susser 1982), while others concede some victory for a short period of time (Piven and Cloward 1977; Fainstein and Fainstein 1974). In some cases, progressive political coalitions form in which local governments work with communities (Clavel 1986; 1991 Monti 1990). Hence, social scientists have analyzed the outcome of issues through the successes and failures of collective protest (Boyte 1980, 1984; Fainstein and Fainstein 1974; Gamson 1975; Hofrichter 1993; Lyman 1995; Morris and Mueller 1992; Oberschall 1973, 1978; Olson 1965; Piven and Cloward 1977; Tilly 1978).

With some exceptions, research on social movements has not examined the broader, long-term consequences of movements (Moore 1994; Chancer forthcoming) and, for the most part, has not analyzed the ways in which individual, grass roots collective struggles politicize ordinary people. Furthermore, with some exceptions (Bookman and Morgan 1988; Crenson 1983; Haywoode 1991; Krauss 1989; Naples 1998a; 1998b) discourses on political participation have not explored community activism as a construct of political behavior. Fainstein and Fainstein (1974) and Piven and Cloward (1977) recognize the development of political consciousness through the collective struggle of a social movement. Although involvement in social movements is considered political activity, to a large extent, participation in local struggles has not been conceptualized as "doing politics." Piven and Cloward (1977) argue that there are "moments" in which poor people are afforded "opportunities" to push for their interests. These "moments" and, therefore, social movements are rare. Analyses of social movements tend to have a broad focus and do not include detailed accounts of grass roots efforts. It is only at the macro level of social movements that collective protest is viewed as political behavior, not at the micro level of community. However, local, community struggles are part of the everyday experiences of ordinary people. People engage in local actions for all kinds of necessities ranging from the addition of a traffic light on a street corner to tenant management of a building, to altering the city's budget. This is political behavior. These same people may never vote, and may never actively participate in a social movement, but are none the less politically active. Hence, a case study of community activism serves as a microcosm of the everyday struggles of community organizations as agents of social change.

Voting and social movements appear to be the only vehicles through which ordinary people influence policy (Boyte 1980, 1984; Fainstein and Fainstein 1974; Gamson 1975; Oberschall 1973, 1978; Olson 1965; Piven and Cloward 1977; Tilly 1978; Campbell, Converse, and Miller 1960; Nie, Verba, and Petrocik 1976; Wolfinger and Rosenstone 1980; Teixeira 1992). Given the rare occurrence of social movements, the locus of political participation by ordinary people is the electoral process and is believed to be the main way in which they affect policy most of the time (Kleppner 1982).

By focusing primarily on the electorate and social movements, social scientists have missed the involvement of low income people[1] in politics thereby limiting theory on political participation. Theoretical models have moved away from an examination of ongoing local displays of political involvement, such as block and civic associations, and ethnic organizations. The very formation of these grass roots groupings gives "democracy in America" (deTocqueville 1956) its unique character. With their roots in town hall meetings, the earliest form of political participation in America, these associations serve as centers of communication and catalysts for the mobilization of local citizens. Furthermore, the paradigm of political participation is defined mostly by men, who are relatively privileged, and social scientists tend to investigate the way in which those like themselves, are politically active.

The paradigm has, therefore, emphasized voter turn-out, political parties, and union politics, and includes a gender bias.

There is also a class bias in the analyses of political participation. Social science informs us that "the power elite" (Mills 1956) are politically involved in that they influence social policy by their standing in society and by being part of a network which includes policy makers. Elites operate within interlocking directorates. For elites, voting is secondary when attempting to sway public policy. In contrast, research on low income groups has described them as apolitical and apathetic (Rainwater et. al. 1959; Komarovsky 1967; Rubin 1976). Even more recent accounts of community activism by sociologists analyzing the political economy describe low income groups as "difficult to mobilize" (Logan and Molotch 1987, 136). Moreover, urban regime theory (Elkin 1987; Mollenkopf 1992; Sites 1994) and urban sociology in general have moved away from analyzing the role of grass roots efforts in policy development. Schattschneider (1960) takes a different position

> Democracy was made for the people, not the people for democracy. Democracy is something for ordinary people, a political system designed to be sensitive to the needs of ordinary people regardless of whether or not the pedants approve of them. It is an outrage to attribute the failures of American democracy to the ignorance and stupidity of the masses. The most disastrous shortcomings of the system have been those of the intellectuals whose concepts of democracy have been amazingly rigid and uninventive...Unless the intellectuals can produce a better theory of politics than they have, it is possible that we shall abolish democracy before we have found out what it is (135-136)!

Most studies investigating the relationship between community power organizations and politics are actually examining the local government structures created in communities to represent residents in City Hall (Thomas 1986; Berry, Portney, and Thomson 1993; Pecorella 1994). Few sociologists and political scientists have recognized the importance of neighborhood life and community organizations in the politicization of low income people. Katznelson (1982) argues that Americans make a distinction between the politics of work and the politics of community, and emphasize ethnicity, race, and territoriality over class. According to Katznelson, there is a "divided consciousness about class in American society that finds many Americans acting on the basis of the shared solidarities of class at work, but on that of ethnic and territorial affinities in their residential communities" (Katznelson 1982, 19). The political behavior of low income groups is demonstrated in community action. "A remarkable consensus of activists is once again turning to the place of residence rather than to the place of work as the main locus of insurgent activity" (Katznelson 1982, 193).

Susser's study of Greenpoint-Williamsburg (1982; 1988) analyzes political activity among the working class. Susser contends that the working class is in a tenuous and vulnerable position in the United States. They are experiencing increasing unemployment because of a reduction of industrial jobs and work opportunities, increasing housing costs, and decreasing benefits. According to Susser, the residents of Greenpoint-Williamsburg responded to these social changes through community struggle. They attempted to prevent further reductions in services and use their block associations as platforms for collective protest. Susser concludes that "protest actions and poor people's movements demonstrate political consciousness and activism among America's working class" (Susser 1982, 209).

This research extends and contributes to the thinking on political behavior among the working class and poor and includes an examination of race relations and gender. This study is done by analyzing the origins, events and issues, and eventual decline of a community organization in Brooklyn called the Greenpoint-Williamsburg Coalition of Community Organizations (GWCOCO). The neighborhoods of Greenpoint and Williamsburg make up northern Brooklyn. Greenpoint is a primarily white, working class area, while Williamsburg is comprised mostly of poor Hispanics and African Americans. These two neighborhoods made up the Coalition. The GWCOCO was a grass roots, multi-ethnic, racially mixed community organization, which used a confrontational style of community action. It operated between 1976 and 1982, an earlier period of fiscal austerity in New York City. From its inception, the organization's purpose was community unity and activism. The Coalition mobilized working class and poor residents of Greenpoint and Williamsburg, to work on community issues. Its mission overtly supported the organization of membership across race, ethnic, religious, class, and gender divisions. Coalition members from each neighborhood bridged their ethnic and racial differences; they worked together to improve and protect their quality of life by fighting for municipal and social services in these communities. The objectives of the Coalition are in line with Tilly's (1978) presentation of various forms of collective actions namely, competitive, reactive, and proactive. "Competitive actions lay claim to resources also claimed by other groups which the actor defines as rivals, competitors, or at least as participants in the same contest...Reactive actions consist of group efforts to reassert established claims when someone else challenges or violates them...Proactive collective actions assert group claims which have not previously been exercised" (Tilly 1978, 144-147). The organizing efforts of the GWCOCO fit all three classifications. Through the Coalition, the Greenpoint-Williamsburg community competed with other New York City neighborhoods for services. The community was also reactive to government and corporate actions and policy decisions. In addition, the GWCOCO mobilized proactive collective actions by raising consciousness about ways in which the quality of life in the community could be improved. Examples of these are the formation of merchants' associations and the restoration and beautification of local parks. This analysis bridges the types of collective actions discussed by Tilly and suggests that the boundary between ordinary people's everyday life and the conceptualization of political activity is clouded by this case.

Membership in the Coalition was through a local community organization, such as block, tenant, and civic associations, as well as religious, health, and housing groups. Political clubs were not accepted as members so that the Coalition's work would not be directed or dominated by local party politicians. In addition, politicians were often the target of the Coalition's actions. By excluding them and their clubs from membership, the GWCOCO would frequently hold them accountable for their performance. The Coalition was made up of approximately 100 community groups.

A second focus of this book is the political participation of low income women. The conventional perception is that women in general, and low income women in particular are apolitical (Rainwater et. al. 1959; Rubin 1976). A long held belief was that women were not politically informed and, therefore, voted the same way as their husbands voted. Like the research on political participation, the analysis of women's political involvement has focused on voter turn-out and the gender gap (Klein 1984). Currently, American women are voting at the same rates as men. However, women vote and view issues differently than men (Klein 1984). During the 1996 Presidential campaign, polls indicated that women gravitated toward the Democratic Party, while men were more inclined to be Republicans (Toner, 1996). Furthermore, women tend to be more supportive and protective of social programs, human services and human rights than men (Nagourney, 1996). Again, with the focus primarily on electoral politics, a male paradigm in the social sciences, women's community activism, for the most part, has not been considered political behavior. Women of Greenpoint-Williamsburg became active in the Coalition and used the organization to maintain and improve the quality of life in the community. Although these women asserted traditional values, such as safety for family, and quality education for children, their tactics at times were unexpected, unorthodox and, hence, intentionally shocking. They were politicized by the process of community action and empowerment.

Feminism informs this analysis. Feminist theorists have gone "beyond white male trade unionism to explore a wider range of political activities, including women's community activism" (Morgen 1988, 97). Feminist scholars have reconceptualized the notion of political behavior (Ackelsberg 1988; Bookman and Morgen 1988; Hardy-Fanta 1993; Haywoode 1991; Krauss 1993; Naples 1991; Pardo 1990). They document women as the organizers of rent strikes (Castells 1983; Lawson and Barton 1980), and activists who prevent the demolition of housing and cuts in municipal services (Susser 1982; 1988). Women have also mobilized against low wages, child molestation, war shortages (Kaplan 1982; West and Blumberg 1990), racism (Naples 1988; 1992), and the dumping of toxic waste (Gibbs 1982; Krauss 1993). Furthermore, women are responsible for forming community organizations and pushing for social welfare and expanded services (Seifer 1976; McCourt 1977; Gelb and Gittell 1986; Luttrell 1988; Ui 1991).

According to these theorists, political behavior is not solely based on the formation of or affiliation with a political party, or by participation in the electoral process. It includes a much broader collection of activities. Community activism is viewed as political behavior. "...political life is community life; politics is attending to the quality of life in households, communities, and workplaces" (Ackelsberg 1988, 308). This analysis also contributes to the literature on women's activism. Although the Coalition was not exclusively a women's organization, women are found as community leaders at much higher rates than in electorally based organizations or clubs. Women forged many local struggles and were elected to executive offices of the Coalition, including the positions of President and Vice President, where in some years, they constituted a majority. Women gained political experience through their involvement in the Coalition.

Finally, this book demonstrates that low income people from different racial and ethnic groups can work together in harmony. Residents of Greenpoint-Williamsburg moved beyond blaming each other for social problems, and supported each other in struggle. The social science literature on urban neighborhoods, beginning with Chicago School, demonstrated the persistence of race and ethnicity as an important characteristic of one's identity. Early members of the Chicago School developed a model of ecological segregation (Burgess 1928) which explained the stages of neighborhood change and the maintenance of social distance among groups with different cultural backgrounds. More recently, on a neighborhood level, segregation has been conceptualized as ordered segmentation (Suttles 1968) and the defended neighborhood (Suttles 1972). In actual practice, attempts to maintain separation among people of different ethnic and racial groups have taken the form of restrictive covenants or zones (Krase 1982), acts of violence (Reider 1986), and the use of local networks (DeSena 1990). The literature has given little attention to community co-operation. The focus of most studies has been on competition and conflict among various ethnic and racial groups who reside in urban neighborhoods (DeSena 1990; Kornblum 1974; Krase 1982; Molotch 1972; Reider 1985; Susser 1982; Suttles 1968). The conflict and competition, for the most part, have been over "turf" and other limited resources, such as housing, jobs, and municipal services. This study illustrates the potential of community organizations in promoting community co-operation and social unity among various ethnic and racial groups. Kornblum (1974) asserts in his study of steelworkers in South Chicago that ethnic and racial differences continue to divide the American working class. However, Kornblum regards neighborhood institutions as having the greatest potential for breaking down the barriers that exist among the working class. This study of the GWCOCO illustrates the potential of community organizations in promoting community co-operation and social unity among various ethnic and racial groups. The Coalition not only raised political consciousness, but also challenged participants' perceptions of race and ethnicity. Coalition members of different ethnic groups came to view each other as allies, with shared interests and common enemies. They moved beyond blaming each other for local problems, and supported each other in struggle. The commitment to create the GWCOCO included an overt dedication to multi-ethnic leadership and participation. The process of overcoming racial and ethnic barriers was handled with finesse by GWCOCO's leaders and staff. They were successful in this endeavor because they respected existing local organizations as vehicles for membership, and understood old divisions. They were able to focus people on common enemies who were decision and policy makers, and convey that these elites were the source of the community's problems.

This study shows that the collective mobilization of low-income groups occurs on a local level. As Castells (1983) suggests, "people appear to have no other choice" (Castells 1983, 329). According to Castells, the city presently represents the state in the minds of ordinary people. "...The citizens in all cases think the national state is too far removed from their problems" (Castells 1983, 330). Attempts to build multi-ethnic and mixed class, national coalitions ignore the importance of commencing by promoting relationships among diverse groups at the grass roots level. Local efforts have the advantage of using the geographic proximity of diverse populations which exist in most cities. It is also in neighborhoods that the problems of society are negotiated by ordinary people who engage in maintaining community on a daily basis. National coalitions would benefit from investing in local communities. This point is best illustrated by the grass roots organizing efforts of both, unions and the Christian Right during the 1996 election.

In summary, this research on the GWCOCO advances a broader perspective on politics. By focusing on community activism this analysis bridges theoretically the areas of political participation, community studies, race and ethnic relations, and feminism. Examining citizen action on a local level offers an alternative and re-conceptualization of political behavior. In essence, it shows that low income groups are not apolitical and apathetic, but rather express political behavior through their activism in which they attempt to control life in their neighborhoods. Community activism is another way in which ordinary people participate in politics and become political. Although ordinary people may not define their activism as political, and are more likely to believe that their community involvement is civic work (Naples 1991) or extensions of household responsibilities (Pardo 1990), they are in fact engaging in local political activity. An outcome for those groups empowered by political action is the raising or deepening of political consciousness (Brecher 1972; DeMartini 1983; Freudenberg and Kohn 1982; Krauss 1989; Morgen 1988). Leaders of the GWCOCO were politicized by their experience of community struggle. Furthermore, I argue that community activism and building coalitions raise political, race, and feminist consciousness which, in turn, can influence the involvement of low income people in electoral politics.

The conclusions of this study include both theoretical and practical implications. First, this research suggests that community activist efforts compose an additional form of political participation. The analysis also indicates the potential of community organizations as agents of political socialization and social change by fostering a critical consciousness among ordinary people. Residents of Greenpoint-Williamsburg were surprised by the lack of responsiveness of government and corporations to their needs when presented with community concerns through a legitimate system. Citizens experienced a contradiction between their belief in a democratic system and the actual workings of the system. Community organizations can direct people's revelations and develop tactics which would require the system to address the community's needs. Through this process of strategy and struggle, people's awareness of politics is altered.

A second theoretical contribution is that the GWCOCO's model of collective actions offers a hybrid of Tilly's (1978) formulation which was discussed earlier. The Coalition mobilized actions which were, in fact, competitive, reactive, and proactive. In most instances, the GWCOCO was advancing issues, which exemplified each of these types, at the same time.

The political participation of low income women is reconceptualized by this analysis. Low income women are political, a notion which challenges conventional wisdom. Their political behavior involves a broader array of activities than voting and the gender gap. The following chapters will discuss the activism of low income women. Through the process of community struggle, women's community work became more visible as they moved into formal roles at public forums. And with every assertion, they were empowered.

This research also demonstrates the possibility of the enhancement of race relations in urban neighborhoods. An earlier analysis of Greenpoint (DeSena 1990) describes the use of informal strategies by residents to "protect turf." In this book, however, I show how many of these same people join with their neighbors of color from Williamsburg to find solutions to local problems. Through the realization of shared problems and a common class position, people of different ethnic backgrounds were able to transcend their ethnocentrism and work together. Every positive experience led to better race relations. Subsequent chapters document how people of different cultural roots worked together for a common good, and in some cases formed lasting friendships and romantic relationships which continue to exist. This new network is called upon to mobilize the community for action, and in local election campaigns. The social science literature and public opinion are, for the most part, void of paradigms which exhibit positive race relations.

Finally, on both a theoretical and practical level, this ethnography raises a concern regarding the future of democracy in the United States. The continued decline of voter turn-out in elections suggests a crisis in representative democracy. Since the demise of local political machines, residents of urban neighborhoods are no longer mobilized around party politics and the electoral process. They are less and less inclined to campaign, vote, and recruit others to vote. Citizens are expressing a need for a more participatory form of democracy by their boycott of the electoral process. They view community activism as a more viable form of politics. By ignoring community organizations and grass roots activities in the overall political process, American political institutions encourage a continuous cycle of declining electoral participation by low income people. Political parties and social movements would profit by the dedication of resources to neighborhood organizing initiatives as an effective strategy to reconnect with their constituencies.

This analysis continues with Chapter 2 which presents demographic and ethnographic descriptions of Greenpoint and Williamsburg as well as an examination of local politics. A comparison of these neighborhoods is also performed. Demographic data from 1980 and 1990 are presented. Although this study presents data from 1990, the patterns discussed were similar during the period of the Coalition's existence. Changes in the community since the decline of the Coalition are also discussed. Chapter 3 discusses the tradition of activism and advocacy programs in existence in the community prior to the emergence of the Coalition. This chapter also indicates that prior to a coalition, Greenpoint and Williamsburg functioned as two separate neighborhoods and racial boundaries were rarely crossed. Finally, Chapter 3 shows the level of social organization in the community which made possible the formation of a coalition of community organizations. Chapter 4 discusses the history and development of the Greenpoint-Williamsburg Coalition of Community Organizations. It describes how the organization was structured to include as members all major racial and ethnic groups residing in Greenpoint-Williamsburg, and to have each group represented on the board of directors. This chapter also discusses the way in which the hiring of an organizing staff included race and ethnic balance representing the composition of the community. Chapter 5 examines various struggles that the organization confronted which includes individual area issues as well as coalition wide issues. The process of struggle heightened people's awareness of and involvement in politics. This chapter indicates the political transformation made by the Coalition's members. Chapter 6 presents the Coalition's decline and discusses how racial differences were used divisively when staff lay offs became necessary. Chapter 7 analyzes the current state of the community without the Coalition and explores a legacy of community control by examining the role of New York City's Community Boards. It suggests how conflicts between people of different racial\ethnic groups, who are members of the Community Board, would be managed by the Coalition. Chapter 8 describes women's informal and formal political activities in the community. It describes women as the initiators and brokers of local issues and problems. This chapter shows how women put aside cultural differences and cross racial\ethnic boundaries, and suggests the feminization of neighborhood life. Finally, Chapter 9 draws conclusions on the potential and effects that community organizations, like the Coalition, have on the political participation and race consciousness of ordinary people and on neighborhood life. It also indicates the importance of resource investment in local areas by those interested in creating national coalitions which connect people of different races, ethnic groups, religions, classes, genders, and sexual orientations.

Notes

[1]. Low income is used to include working class and poor people.

CHAPTER 2

THE NEIGHBORHOODS

The neighborhoods of Greenpoint and Williamsburg comprise the peninsula of northern Brooklyn, one of the five boroughs of New York City. In 1990, Brooklyn had a population of 2,300,664[1] and is divided into eighteen Community Boards[2]. Geographically, Greenpoint extends from the East River and Newtown Creek to the Brooklyn-Queens Expressway and North 7th Street (New York City Planning Commission 1969). Greenpoint is a primarily white, working class area, made up mostly of Poles, Italians, Hispanics, and Irish residents. Williamsburg begins at Greenpoint's southern boundary and continues south to Flushing Avenue. Williamsburg has more ethnic minorities than Greenpoint in that it is comprised mostly of Italian, Hispanic, African American, and Hasidic Jewish communities.

Greenpoint-Williamsburg was purchased from the Canarsie Indians by the Dutch West India Company in 1638. The areas of Greenpoint, Williamsburg, and Bushwick constituted the Township of Bushwick which was under the jurisdiction of Peter Stuyvesant.[3] In the late 1830's, Greenpoint was linked to Williamsburg and Bushwick by a 19th century highway called Franklin Turnpike. The Greenpoint-Williamsburg community was later connected to Manhattan's lower east side by the Williamsburg Bridge. "This facilitated the movement of workers and industry to Greenpoint-Williamsburg and other parts of Brooklyn" (Susser 1982, 23). Presently, Greenpoint-Williamsburg has bridges, highways, buses, and subway trains which unite the community with the rest of Brooklyn, Queens, and Manhattan.

Greenpoint and Williamsburg differ from each other when a number of variables are considered, namely race, age, income, education, occupation, housing type, occupancy, and gross rents. Census data from 1980 and 1990 are discussed. The demographic patterns presented describe the neighborhoods during the Coalition's existence. Recent population changes are also documented.

In 1980, Greenpoint-Williamsburg had a population of 142,942. Of these residents, 49 percent were white (non Hispanic) 7 percent black (non Hispanic), 42 percent were of Hispanic origin, and 2 percent were "other." These compare to 1990 demographics in which the population increased 9 percent and 46 percent were white (non Hispanic), 7 percent were black (non Hispanic), 44 percent were Hispanic, and 3 percent were "other" (Population Change by Race and Hispanic origin by Selected Ages; Housing Unit Change, Brooklyn Community District 1, 1980-1990).

Williamsburg is geographically and demographically larger than Greenpoint.[4] In 1990, the total population of Williamsburg was 114,586 compared to 39,365 living in Greenpoint.[5] Williamsburg also contains more people of color than Greenpoint. In 1990, Greenpoint's population was 73 percent white (non Hispanic), 1 percent black (non Hispanic), 4 percent Asian and Pacific Islander (non Hispanic), and 22 percent Hispanic. During the 1980's, Greenpoint experienced a dramatic influx of immigrants from Poland, who have been successful at establishing themselves in the area. In addition to some retail chain establishments, such as Genovese Drugs and Parade of Shoes, stores along the main retail strip of Manhattan and Nassau Avenues are mostly Polish, selling ethnic food, clothing, and accessories. Retailers in jewelry, leather apparel, herbs and homeopathy, and skin and nail care salons have increased with the immigrant population. Polish is heard as you walk the streets, and merchants greet customers in Polish. In addition, old time merchants employ Polish speaking sales persons. The local schools are realizing the presence of these immigrants as their children apply for admission. Greenpoint is often presently referred to as "Little Warsaw," a reference to the capital of Poland.

Williamsburg, on the other hand, was 37 percent white (non Hispanic and probably mostly Hasidim), 10 percent black (non Hispanic), 2 percent Asian and Pacific Islander (non Hispanic), and 51 percent Hispanic. More recently, Williamsburg is experiencing a growing community of artists who find residence in Manhattan too expensive. It is estimated that between 2,000 and 3,000 artists are presently exhibiting in Williamsburg.[6] They have converted loft buildings, which have been abandoned because of a decline in manufacturing, into working studios and living space. Williamsburg is a convenient location for artists because it offers close proximity to Manhattan's lower east side. It is one subway stop on the L train from Bedford Avenue in Williamsburg to First Avenue and 14th Street in Manhattan. The presence of artists has precipitated the establishment of gourmet, vegetarian, and ethnic restaurants such as Mexican and Thai, all of which introduce new cuisines to the Greenpoint-Williamsburg community.

The rate of births in Greenpoint-Williamsburg remained the same in 1990 as in 1980, 21 per 1000 (Vital Statistics, Brooklyn Community District 1). Williamsburg's population is younger than that of Greenpoint. In 1990, 35 percent of Williamsburg's population was under 18 years of age compared to 17 percent in Greenpoint.[7] One also sees many babies and young children in Greenpoint, many of whom are the offspring of Polish immigrants and gentrifiers.

Greenpoint-Williamsburg is best described as a low income area. In 1980, 28 percent of residents of Greenpoint-Williamsburg had incomes from public assistance, social security, or medicaid. This number increased to 32 percent in 1990 (Income Support, Brooklyn Community District 1). In general, Williamsburg is a poorer neighborhood than Greenpoint. Williamsburg's average of median household income in 1989 was $16,884 compared to Greenpoint's $29,121. In addition, Williamsburg's households received more of their income from public assistance than those in Greenpoint. In 1989, 29 percent of households in Williamsburg received public assistance compared to 10 percent of Greenpoint's households. Moreover, Greenpoint had a slightly higher proportion of households receiving social security income in 1989. Twenty-eight percent of the households in Greenpoint collected social security income, compared with 24 percent of those in Williamsburg. This is most likely attributed to an older population in Greenpoint.

Greenpoint's residents achieved a somewhat higher level of formal education than those in Williamsburg. Considering persons 25 years and older in 1990 who lived in Greenpoint, 17 percent had less than a 9th grade education, 22 percent realized grades 9 through 12, but acquired no diploma, 30 percent were high school graduates or obtained an equivalency diploma, 12 percent attended some college, but held no degree, 5 percent completed an Associate's degree, 8 percent a Bachelor's degree, and 6 percent held a graduate or professional degree. These demographics compare to Williamsburg's residents who were 25 years or older in 1990 in which 31 percent had less than a 9th grade education (more than in Greenpoint), 28 percent realized grades 9 through 12, but acquired no diploma (more than in Greenpoint), 24 percent were high school graduates or obtained an equivalency diploma (less than in Greenpoint), 9 percent attended some college, but held no degree (less than in Greenpoint), 3 percent completed an Associate's degree (less than in Greenpoint), 4 percent a Bachelor's degree (less than in Greenpoint), and 2 percent held a graduate or professional degree (less than in Greenpoint).

The occupations of residents in Greenpoint and Williamsburg were also somewhat dissimilar. In terms of employed persons 16 years and older in 1990, Greenpoint had more professionals and managers (20 percent) than Williamsburg (16 percent). In addition, Greenpoint had more residents in precision production, craft and repair occupations (14 percent) than Williamsburg (10 percent). In contrast, Williamsburg had more operators, fabricators,and laborers (24 percent) than Greenpoint (18 percent). Both neighborhoods reported approximately the same proportion of people employed in technical, sales, and administrative support occupations (30 percent in Greenpoint and 32 percent in Williamsburg), and service (17 percent in Greenpoint and 18 percent in Williamsburg).

Greenpoint and Williamsburg are physically disparate as well, although both areas show signs of deterioration, due to age and poor maintenance by City government. In terms of housing, Williamsburg has a larger proportion of buildings with multiple units, while Greenpoint's buildings tend to be smaller and have fewer units than in Williamsburg. Total housing units in Greenpoint-Williamsburg increased only 1 percent from 1980 (Total Housing Units, Brooklyn Community District 1). In 1990, 1 percent of buildings in Greenpoint had one detached unit, 2 percent had one attached unit, 13 percent had two units, 28 percent had three or four units, 45 percent had five to nine units, 6 percent had ten to nineteen units, 3 percent had twenty to forty-nine units, 1 percent had fifty or more units, while 1 percent had another type of housing. As previously stated, there are more larger buildings in Williamsburg. In 1990, 1 percent of structures in Williamsburg had one detached unit, 2 percent had one attached unit, 10 percent had two units, 18 percent had three or four units, 18 percent had five to nine units, 8 percent had ten to nineteen units, 20 percent had twenty to forty-nine units, 22 percent had fifty or more units, and 1 percent had another type of housing. These data have taken into account the fact that Williamsburg is also home to a number of housing developments managed by New York City's Housing Authority namely, Cooper Park Houses, Taylor-Whyte Houses, Roberto

Clemente Plaza, Johnathan Williams Houses, Independence Tower. In contrast there are no government sponsored housing developments in Greenpoint. In Greenpoint there is a seven block historic district which includes churches, synagogues, commercial establishments and houses which are remnants of Dutch settlement and 19th century architecture. Furthermore, Greenpoint had more owner occupied housing units than Williamsburg. In 1990, 21 percent of Greenpoint's units were owner occupied compared to 11 percent in Williamsburg. Conversely, 79 percent of Greenpoint's units were renter occupied, while 89 percent of housing units in Williamsburg were renter occupied. Finally, rental units cost more in Greenpoint than in Williamsburg. In 1990, the average of median gross rents in Greenpoint was $450 compared to $378 in Williamsburg. Rents, however, have been escalating dramatically in the Northside portion of Williamsburg which is home to many artists and professionals. Advertisements related to apartments and lofts in the Northside and historic Greenpoint quote rents at $1,000 to $1,500 monthly.

An examination of these neighborhoods compared to New York City as a whole, adds another level of description to this analysis and places these neighborhoods within the context of the city of which it is a part. In 1990, Greenpoint was comprised of more whites (non Hispanic) than New York City (43 percent), and New York City was made up of more whites (non Hispanic) than Williamsburg. In addition, New York City contained more blacks (non Hispanic), amounting to 26 percent, than both Greenpoint and Williamsburg. Williamsburg had twice as many Hispanics than Greenpoint and New York City (24 percent).

In terms of income, Greenpoint more closely reflected New York City than Williamsburg. In 1989, the median household income for New York City was $29,823. Williamsburg is poorer than both Greenpoint and the City as a whole. It follows, therefore, that Williamsburg had the highest percentage of residents receiving public assistance, while 13 percent of New York City's population obtained public assistance. In comparison, Greenpoint had the lowest proportion of residents collecting public assistance. However, Greenpoint had the most people receiving social security income. Williamsburg and New York City (25 percent) had about the same proportion of residents claiming social security income in 1989.

An analysis of formal education brings informative results. As previously discussed, Greenpoint and Williamsburg exhibit some differences on this variable. When both are compared to New York City, results show that Williamsburg had the largest number of residents who did not complete high school, while New York City had the largest proportion of people with Bachelor's degrees (12 percent) and graduate and professional degrees (10 percent).

In comparing these three areas regarding occupation, the 1990 Census reveals that there were more professionals and managers in New York City (31 percent) than in Greenpoint and Williamsburg. Concurrently, there were more operators, fabricators, and laborers in Greenpoint and Williamsburg than in New York City which totaled 12 percent.

In 1990, New York City had the highest proportion of owner occupied (29 percent) housing relative to Greenpoint and Williamsburg, while Williamsburg had the lowest. However, Williamsburg had the largest amount of renter occupied housing units, followed by Greenpoint and New York City respectively. Finally, rental housing cost more in New York City as a whole than in Greenpoint and Williamsburg. In 1990, the median gross rent in New York City was $496. Rental housing in Williamsburg was the cheapest.

Greenpoint-Williamsburg is home to many churches and synagogues. Those in Greenpoint with the largest congregations are Catholic. In Williamsburg, various other Christian churches and synagogues also exist. The Catholic churches are smaller because of the residence of Hasidim and competition with Pentecostal churches and Jehovah's Witnesses for congregants. Religious services reflect the ethnic group which is dominant. Services are offered in Spanish, Polish, Hebrew, and Yiddish, as well as English. Churches and synagogues are reminders of 19th century immigrant groups, such as Germans and eastern Europeans, who were first to settle in northern Brooklyn. "Orthodox Jews had lived in Williamsburg since the 1800's. In the 1940's large numbers of Hasidim and other religious Jewish sects, fleeing persecution in Europe, followed influential rabbis to establish a strong community in Williamsburg" (Susser 1982, 24-25). Those settling in Brooklyn after World War II were survivors of the Holocaust. The southwest section of Williamsburg is home to the largest Hasidic sect, the Satmar (Abrahamson 1996; Kranzler 1995). Presently, there are approximately 50,000[8] Hasidim living in Williamsburg.

Although New York City's government agencies have arrived at clear boundaries between the neighborhoods, residents do not express the same exactness. People residing within the City's boundaries for Greenpoint know that they live in Greenpoint. However, there is a tendency for white, non-Hispanic groups, such as Italians and Poles, who live in Williamsburg according to the City's definition, to define their place of residence as Greenpoint or Greenpoint-Williamsburg. According to one resident,

> I think this is Williamsburg, although we live right near Greenpoint, but I think it is Williamsburg according to the zip code. I say Greenpoint because I feel I do come from Greenpoint because I'm so near the heart of Greenpoint...I say this is Greenpoint because I don't want everyone thinking of the south side of Williamsburg.

The respondent's reference to the south side of Williamsburg indicates concern about being associated with a largely Hispanic community made up mostly of old tenement buildings. These are negative attributes for this respondent. Another resident expressed,

> Greenpoint-Williamsburg, that's what I usually say. We're on a borderline, actually I live in Williamsburg. But you see with Williamsburg, they always affiliate it with the area past Grand Street which is a mess, and I have a little residential pride so I usually say Greenpoint-Williamsburg for that reason.

It appears that naming one's place of residence is an exercise in "impression management" (Goffman 1959). Williamsburg is presently viewed as a "stigmatized place" (Krase 1979) because of the presence of minority groups including Hasidim. Consequently, many white, non-Hispanic residents resolve the contradiction between their place of residence and the stigma attached to it by identifying with Greenpoint or associating themselves with it by using a hyphenated Greenpoint-Williamsburg. In either case, their attempt is to attach to an area they perceive as the "better" one in that it is mostly white, non-Hispanic, with smaller buildings, and a more manicured appearance. This practice also illustrates one form of "fusion" discussed by Hunter (1974). It is an attempt to borrow the name and thereby the prestige of an adjacent area. Although Greenpoint is not a highly prestigious neighborhood, it is perceived to be more prestigious than Williamsburg. These respondents, who represent many Williamsburg residents, are attempting to rid themselves of the negative ideas associated with Williamsburg. In essence, they see themselves outside the physical boundaries of

Greenpoint, but inside Greenpoint's symbolic boundaries. Williamsburg's image is changing with the residence of artists and other professionals. It is now considered vogue and chic to live to live on the Northside (and parts of the Southside).

As the Coalition was forming, it divided the neighborhoods into six areas to insure that the interests of various ethnic and racial groups were represented. These areas were: Greenpoint (white, mixed ethnic groups), Northside (Polish), Central Williamsburg (Italian and African Americans), East Williamsburg (African Americans and Hispanics), Southside (Hispanic), South Williamsburg (Hasidic Jews and Hispanics, however the Hasidic community was not a regular participant in the Coalition). As part of the Coalition's organizational structure, each section elected three vice presidents to represent it as well as voted for the Executive Board, which consisted of President, Executive Vice President, Secretary, and Treasurer. Elections took place at an annual convention, and vacancies were filled at delegate assemblies, which were held four times a year.

The neighborhoods of Greenpoint-Williamsburg also make up Brooklyn's Community Board 1. Community Boards are districts by which New York City is divided. New York City's Charter mandates coterminality between Community Boards and service districts.[9] In other words, services such as sanitation, police, and fire protection are decentralized and function within service areas. The boundaries for service coincide with those of the Community Board. The population of each Board varies because the boundaries have remained constant to support coterminality. Boards are comprised of a maximum of fifty people, half of whom are appointed by the Borough President and the other half are appointed by representatives comprising the City Council. Community Boards serve as agents of City government within the community and operate as liaisons between communities and City government. An extensive analysis of the function of community boards and a comparison between Brooklyn's Community Board 1 and GWCOCO is discussed further in Chapter 7.

Local electoral politics in Greenpoint-Williamsburg unites the various ethnic communities into the 50th Assembly District. Greenpoint-Williamsburg has been a long time bastion of the Democratic Party. Local politicians emerge from the Seneca Club, an organization of regular Democrats. In particular, District Leaders and representatives to the City Council and State Assembly and Senate are members of the Seneca Club. Residents of Greenpoint-Williamsburg do vote for

Republicans above the level of local representatives. For example, the community supported Ronald Reagan for President in 1984[10], and Rudolph Guiliani for Mayor in 1993[11]. If the neighborhoods are examined separately, one finds that Williamsburg tends to vote for Democratic Party candidates more consistently than Greenpoint, and voters in Greenpoint will cross party lines in elections more readily than those in Williamsburg. For example, in the last Mayoral election, David Dinkins (the Democratic incumbent who is African American) carried the communities of color within Williamsburg, and U.S. Senator Alphonse D'Amato does well in Greenpoint. However, the majority of constituents in both neighborhoods are registered Democrats. In 1992, Bill Clinton carried the area in the Presidential race, while D'Amato was supported by voters in Greenpoint.

In analyzing voter turn-out by ethnicity in Greenpoint-Williamsburg, one finds that the communities of color have the lowest rate, followed by white residents. The Hasidim vote at the highest rate. They vote as a block for the candidate sanctioned by the rebbe, and go to the polls in response to the rebbe's suggestion. During elections, the Hasidim are referred to as the "late vote," since they leave to vote at around 7:30 PM after religious services, and usually keep the polling place open until 10:00 or 11:00 PM. Polls close in New York at 9:00 PM. Like the other constituencies in the community, the Hasidim are Democrats, but elected Guiliani and D'Amato. They are also the major constituents of the local City Councilman and District Leader, and are members of the Seneca Club. They behave as a political force, and politicians seeking election pay homage to the rebbe. The Hasidim understand power relations, and have realized a position of power in New York politics.

In general, like the nation, Greenpoint-Williamsburg has a low level of participation and voter turn-out is on the decline. Reapportionment has not been kind to the community and the community has essentially been balkanized. A separate election district was formed to give the communities of color political representation. The remaining portions of the community are part of a larger district with areas of Manhattan and other neighborhoods in Brooklyn. Presently, the community is not seriously considered by some of its representatives because there is no core constituency for them in Greenpoint-Williamsburg, and there is a lack of activism and diminishing turn-out. These politicians give most of their attention to supporters in Brooklyn Heights and Manhattan's east side. If it were still in existence, the Coalition would hold these politicians accountable for their dismissal of the community.

There are many community organizations in Greenpoint-Williamsburg. In 1975, a funded employment program under the federal government's Comprehensive Employment and Training Act (CETA) was obtained by the community. The number of community organizations dramatically increased in order to utilize the entire CETA grant. The workings of a CETA grant in the community will be discussed in greater detail in Chapter 3. CETA and non CETA organizations made up the Coalition. By 1981, community organizations began to decline. Ronald Reagan was President, and the federal government was slashing grants to communities. Many community organizations in Greenpoint-Williamsburg went out of business. By 1982, this roster included the Coalition. The decline of the Coalition and an analysis of those organizations which survived the Reagan years will be discussed in Chapter 6.

Given the demographic and ethnographic differences between Greenpoint and Williamsburg, the question arises as to why these communities would organize a coalition? The initial funding source of this project, the Campaign for Human Development of the Catholic Conference of Bishops, was committed to the empowerment of ordinary people. Greenpoint-Williamsburg was a plausible site because the two neighborhoods made-up the Community Board, were low income, and exhibited clear ethnic\racial diversity. Originally, the idea to organize a community coalition was a social experiment of sorts. The Coalition's founders and staff invested their time and energy, and effectively enlisted member groups by indicating that it was in the organization's self interest to join the Coalition. Many community groups in Greenpoint and Williamsburg realized the importance of forming and participating in a coalition. Members eventually discerned that government and corporations were not to be trusted, and that the neighborhoods themselves did not need to be rivals. Through participation in actions, many learned that blaming others, particularly from different ethnic\racial groups, was not the solution to improving their conditions. In fact, members ultimately realized that they had similar community problems, which often focused on scarcity. Many were able to transcend their differences, recognize commonalities, and confront the neighborhoods' adversaries in unity, which empowered the Coalition, and community residents. The process of participating in a multi-ethnic coalition, which engaged in community struggles with the power elite, altered and raised the political and race consciousness of many residents in Greenpoint-Williamsburg. People were transformed by this process.

Notes

[1] The demographics reported were obtained by analyzing the census tracts from the 1990 Census of Population and Housing.

[2] The number of Community Boards was obtained from the Brooklyn NYNEX White Pages, 1996-1997.

[3] "Greenpoint" unpublished pamphlet, sponsored by the Brooklyn Union Gas Company, p.1.

[4] Thirty-five census tracts comprise Williamsburg, while seventeen make up Greenpoint.

[5] The demographics reported were obtained by analyzing census tracts from the 1990 Census of Population and Housing, Summary Tape File 3A.

[6] This information was obtained from the Brooklyn Waterfront Artist Coalition.

[7] "Percent of Population Under 18 Years of Age," compiled profile of Brooklyn Community Board 1.

[8] This information was obtained from James Barron, Sale of a Grand Rabbi's Home Is Upheld. The New York Times, Wednesday, July 3, 1996, p. B3.

[9] City of New York, New York City Charter, as Amended October 31, 1992.

[10] The New York Times, November 7, 1984.

[11] The New York Times, November 3, 1993.

CHAPTER 3

THE SOCIAL CLIMATE

Greenpoint-Williamsburg has long been a bastion of the Democratic Party regarding electoral politics. In terms of a broader conceptualization of political participation, Greenpoint-Williamsburg also has a tradition of activism. Before discussing the emergence of the Greenpoint-Williamsburg Coalition of Community Organizations, this chapter will first examine the history of the area with regard to community organizing. In Greenpoint-Williamsburg, attempts were made to stop industrial expansion, and the closing of a firehouse. In addition, the community has a history of advocacy efforts, such as anti-poverty programs, day care and senior centers, and employment programs. This chapter will discuss the community's tradition of activism, and show how this history helped to foster the eventual development of the Greenpoint-Williamsburg Coalition of Community Organizations.

ANTI-POVERTY PROGRAMS

In 1964, President Johnson called for "a war on poverty in America" (Piven and Cloward 1977, 270). The Economic Opportunity Act (EOA) of 1964 expanded services initiated by the Johnson Administration and built upon some small programs established during the Kennedy years. The war on poverty was waged through anti-poverty programs. Between 1965 and 1967, funding was obtained through the Office of Economic Opportunity. In Greenpoint-Williamsburg, these service programs were distributed through the Williamsburg Community Corporation. Joe,[1] a social service worker in Williamsburg explained,

> Community corporations were the forerunners to the
> Community Development Agency and Area Policy Boards,
> and those elections were the first time that community people
> could run against the organization. The Williamsburg
> Community Corporation included Greenpoint. A coalition of
> black and Hispanic churches [in Williamsburg] won the first
> community election and elected a Lutheran priest president
> of the Corporation. The reason we won is because the
> election took place in the summer, and the Hasidics weren't
> here. It was one of the few times we were able to defeat the
> Hasidics. The more radical community groups in the area
> defeated the political party, the Hasidics, and the Catholic
> Church in Greenpoint which was our power base. That is
> where people got a taste of winning some influence and
> power. A lot of groups emanated from that. That is the
> beginning of community activism and community power in
> this area.

After 1967, there was local control of federal money where community
organizations were funded through State and City agencies. Prior to this,
local groups used federal money to organize against local governments.
In reaction to this pressure, Mayors requested that Congress enact
legislation that would enable the federal government to fund community
groups through local governments. One anti-poverty program was
awarded to the School Settlement Association, which was located in the
Italian section of Williamsburg. The woman who was hired to direct this
program, June Price, was a professional social worker who had recently
moved into the community. She claims, "The white minister who ran the
Settlement House at the time, hired me because of my MSW, but was
nervous about me. I sounded too assertive and too direct for him." It
seems that his instincts were accurate. As director of an anti-poverty
program, June made two observations. First, that there were no Italians
employed at School Settlement, even though it was located in the heart of
an Italian community. Second, that the Board of Directors, which
oversaw the anti-poverty program, did not represent poor people, despite
the fact that this was a requirement for funding. In reality, there were no
poor people, nor Italians on the Board of Directors, but rather, Board
members were actually community elites, people influential in local
politics, and religious institutions. June learned that the absence of Italian
employees and Board members was rooted in a belief at School
Settlement that Italians would not use their services. June believed,

however, that they should disregard this myth and reach out to the Italian community with a first step of hiring Italians.

Within the first few months of June's employment at School Settlement, she was visited by a 15 year old, Italian girl and her parents. The girl was pregnant and her parents were seeking abortion counseling from June. Greenpoint-Williamsburg is a predominantly Catholic community where many children attend elementary schools run by Catholic parishes. Some local social service agencies also hold a pro-life view and prohibit abortion counseling. Although the family sought counseling from June, her employer was not pleased by her giving the family information about abortion. The combination of this incident and the fact that June had verbally criticized the Board of Directors for not meeting the objectives of the war on poverty, led to her termination at School Settlement Association. School Settlement's action led June's staff to take the program's files and walk out with her. According to June, since School Settlement's board of directors was illegal due to the absence of employees and members who could adequately represent the community, the Williamsburg Community Corporation moved the program with June to another community organization, Conselyea Street Block Association. The anti-poverty program was named Education Action Center (EAC). June continued to direct the program, and in her tenure at EAC, she developed many of the social programs in the Greenpoint-Williamsburg community, secured funding, and organized actions to maintain local resources. She explained,

> The more I went around the more I could see that the white, working class really had nothing. Their houses were deteriorating. It was very obvious how people had been institutionally pitted against one another. You could see there's no programs in the Italian community, with people desperately trying to keep their houses going with inflation going up. Here the black and Hispanic communities were getting services. There was a war on poverty, and there was nothing here [in the Italian community].

With this view in mind, June set out to change the institutional perceptions of the white, working class. The remaining discussion in this chapter demonstrates her influence.

CONSELYEA STREET BLOCK ASSOCIATION

In 1967, a group of women who lived on Conselyea Street gathered to discuss a problem they were having with a number of tenement buildings located on Metropolitan Avenue. The backyards of those owning two and three family houses on Conselyea Street were adjacent to the backyards of these tenement buildings. Tenants residing in these tenements were throwing trash out their back windows, and allowing it to collect there. The landlords on Conselyea Street objected to this practice, since it affected the use of their backyards. The women requested assistance from the Williamsburg Community Corporation which responded with the suggestion that they form a block association. This block association became the sponsoring board for Education Action Center (EAC). EAC was Conselyea Street's first funded program. To a large extent, EAC worked with local youths, ran a summer recreation program, was a site for the federal lunch program, and assisted eligible residents to obtain government benefits. This certainly was the public's perception of the program. Behind the scenes, however, June Price was continuing her needs assessment of the community. She realized the need for a day care center and knew that public funding was going to be made available. She reports,

> My view was that we needed to do something. That's one of my strengths, I always think you have to do something. I had this idea of a day care center. I heard that there was money available for child care. I had friends at ACD [Agency for Child Development]. I was trying to think of a way to bring people together across race and ethnic lines. Remember, I was coming from CORE [Congress for Racial Equality].

There was neighborhood opposition to the day care center. In fact, board members of Conselyea Street Block Association received threatening phone calls from residents. Much opposition came from local Italians who believed that they would not be able to use the center. They thought it would service minorities, and therefore bring outsiders into the community. I was told in interviews that Italian residents would call the Agency for Child Development, the funding source, and ask, "can middle class people use day care?" They were told that day care centers are for poor people. The Italian community did not identify or perceive itself as poor or working class, when that was the reality. For them, those who are poor, are people of color. Thus, they did not believe that day care would be available to them. The compromise to the building of a day care center in the Italian section of Williamsburg was that a senior citizens center would also occupy the facility.[2] The Block Association was involved in the design of the facility, and catered to the habits of Italians by including an indoor baci ball[3] court in the senior center. This may also have been an attempt to insure that the senior center would attract and be used by local Italians. The facility opened in 1974 under the names, Small World Day Care Center and Swinging Sixties Senior Citizens Center, sponsored by Conselyea Street Block Association.

S & S CORRUGATED COMPANY

In 1972 S&S Corrugated Paper Machinery Company, a manufacturer of paper boxes, wanted to expand its plant which was located on the Northside[4] of Greenpoint-Williamsburg. "Nineteen houses, the homes for ninety-four families, were to be torn down to make place for a new wing" (Susser 1982, 170) to be added to the factory. In protest of this expansion, residents of the Northside were mobilized by local activists. At this time, June Price owned a house on the Northside which further influenced her to and become involved in this issue, and organize residents to fight for their homes. June explained that the union of community activists which developed to drive this issue was: an urban planner from Pratt Institute, a local undertaker, priests from two Catholic churches on the Northside, and June. To bring attention to the issue and to announce the community's resistance to the planned industrial expansion, residents stopped traffic on the Brooklyn-Queens Expressway during rush hour.[5] They also physically blocked bulldozers which were aimed at demolishing the Northside's homes. A compromise agreement was eventually reached between the community and the City of New York.

> Fourteen three-story homes, designed to house forty-one families, were to be built by New York City on a nearby block. These residential units were classified as "moderate income co-operatives" and had to be purchased, not rented (Susser 1982, 170).

Residents viewed this concession as a major victory, even though only about 20 percent of those displaced actually moved into the new housing

(Susser 1982) and the Northside homes were demolished.

This experience resulted in the formation of a community organization, the Northside Community Development Council (NCDC). NCDC received public funding, hired a small staff, and rented a storefront to work on other quality of life issues on the Northside. In addition, the Young at Heart Senior Citizens Center was established on the Northside shortly after the S&S Corrugated struggle. Those involved in the struggle say that "[The senior center] was a payoff for this battle."

PEOPLE'S FIREHOUSE

In 1975, New York City was experiencing a fiscal crisis. The City's administration, pressured by a State appointed Emergency Financial Control Board, proposed a program of fiscal austerity to resolve fiscal problems. This program translated into cuts in City services. One area affected was New York City's Fire Department, where a number of engine companies were slated for closing. It should be mentioned that these closings occurred at a time when the City was also experiencing increasing cases of arson. Buildings were literally torched and money from fire insurance was collected by owners. In certain areas of the City, such as Bushwich and the south Bronx, city blocks were emptied from arson. Among the firehouses closed was Engine Company 212, which was located on the Northside of Greenpoint-Williamsburg. Since the Northside community had battled and lost housing with S&S Corrugated, they were determined not to be defeated and have any additional services cut.

> The firemen assigned to guard the firehouse promised local residents to sound the siren if they expected the engine to be removed. At 6 P.M. on November 21, 1975, the siren was sounded. The numerous organizations and associations in the area filtered the news among residents by telephone, and within an hour two hundred people surrounded the firehouse. For twenty hours the engine and twenty-four firemen sent to remove it were held hostage, with many of the demonstrators staying all night... Eventually a compromise was reached between [the community and the Commissioner]. The firemen were set free, and the engine remained with the community (Susser 1982, 172).

For a year and a half, residents occupied the firehouse. One family stayed the entire time, however, most took shifts. In addition to this occupation, residents participated in other actions as well. They picketed a mayoral dinner, the home of the fire commissioner, and stopped traffic on the Brooklyn-Queens Expressway during rush hour (Susser 1982). The community never allowed the City to think that it would give up the fight. On March 3, 1977, Engine Company 212 was re-opened. A community organization named People's Firehouse emerged from this struggle.

Residents' knowledge of organizing, illustrated by the cases of S&S Corrugated and People's Firehouse, had its roots in union organizing. Greenpoint, in particular, "is a turn-of-the-century manufacturing town" (Williams and Kornblum 1985, 2). Industries lined the waterfront as well as claiming many streets in the community. Local residents found employment in these firms, which were highly unionized. Residents made a connection between union organizing and community organizing. The union experience and worker's struggles influenced the way in which people in Greenpoint-Williamsburg handled community issues.

CETA CONSORTIUM

In 1974, the federal government agreed to directly fund the non profit sector to provide jobs in social programs under the Comprehensive Employment and Training Act (CETA). The federal government was attempting to deal with a high unemployment rate through CETA by paying people a wage while they acquired on the job training and work experience. This was the first time in the history of CETA in which the federal government considered not for profit community organizations as the recipients of CETA grants. In Greenpoint-Williamsburg, it was June Price who learned that the federal government was going to fund a few demonstration projects in New York City. June's interest in CETA funding was to build the National Congress of Neighborhood Women, a nation wide organization of mostly working class women involved in community activism. She organized a small group of leaders from Greenpoint and Williamsburg to apply for a CETA grant.[6] This group developed a proposal, and decided that fiscal responsibility for the contract would be given to School Settlement Association. School Settlement had a history of managing grants, so this decision, was a practical one from the point of view of the community leaders involved. Not all leaders were happy with this decision however, and one leader, Cindy, remarked, "Conselyea Street will never forgive me, but they were just starting out. School Settlement had money before." Cindy voted for School Settlement as the administrator of the grant even though her loyalty and political alignment was with Conselyea Street Block Association. At the time, no other community organization in Greenpoint-Williamsburg could compete with School Settlement's experience of administering grants. Thus, the proposal was submitted under their name, with the support of community organizations.

In 1975, School Settlement was awarded a $3 million contract under the Comprehensive Employment and Training Act, which included 295 job slots.[7] Cindy expressed, "it happened fast and we had to hire quickly." Jobs, which carried various titles, were distributed to community organizations. In order to award all 295 slots, new community organizations were created. Nearly 12 additional, not for profit organizations emerged for the purpose of satisfying the CETA grant. For example, the local chapter of the Italian American Civil Rights League became the Italian American Multi Service Center, a necessary change in status so that they could receive CETA slots. National Congress of Neighborhood Women began with 25 CETA positions. St. Nicholas Neighborhood Preservation and Housing Rehabilitation Corporation also got their start with CETA jobs. Other organizations also developed in response to the CETA grant, such as Neighborhood Facilities Corporation, People for People, Williamsburg Volunteer Ambulance Corporation. Money for the administration of CETA was part of the funding package. Although community organizations received jobs, they did not receive any other money from the CETA grant. Administrative funds were used by School Settlement Association to hire field and fiscal staff. Most of the other organizations with job slots ran store front operations, but did not have any funds to pay rent or to buy furniture. Most organizations held fundraisers to support their offices. Over time they became resentful that School Settlement did not share any of the administrative money. Cindy further explained,

> The idea with CETA was that it was a coalition. One group would have the money, but we would carefully work out how the money and power would be handled. But over time, [School Settlement] began to pull the jobs and pull the money. The liaison workers were turned into little bureaucrats.

The hiring process was carried out by each individual community organization. CETA, however, set conditions of eligibility and required that only those unemployed or underemployed could be hired for a CETA position. In addition, each job title had particular criteria for employment. For example, the positions of Director, Teacher, and Social Worker required a college degree. The qualifications for a Community Organizer were a high school diploma and experience in community work. Given these requirements, for the most part, employees were hired by a system of patronage, and as Danny, director of a local social service agency described, it was a program of "jobs for a friend." The CETA consortium set the stage for the development of the Greenpoint-Williamsburg Coalition of Community Organizations. The CETA grant put in place a network of community organizations with a paid staff to mobilize around local issues. There was a ready made cadre of member groups and community residents, who were CETA workers, to participate in the Coalition. Because of this unique position, residents, who were community workers, were able to attend meetings and actions during the day or evening, represent the organization for whom they worked at these gatherings, and be paid for their time or receive "comp time."[8] In addition, there were a number of storefronts belonging to member organizations that the Coalition could use for meetings. It is most important to realize that the implementation of Greenpoint-Williamsburg's CETA contract paved the way for the emergence of the Greenpoint-Williamsburg Coalition of Community Organizations. CETA unified home and work which enabled people to organize. The leaders of CETA organizations and their employees saw the Coalition's mission as part of the staff's job descriptions. Furthermore, with a tradition of activism in the community combined with the CETA contract, there was a union which allowed Greenpoint-Williamsburg to engage in ongoing issue organizing in the tradition of Saul Alinsky (1971), and thus, permitted the community to experience and better understand empowerment.

The development of the Coalition as an organization will be discussed in the next chapter. However, it should be noted that Greenpoint-Williamsburg's CETA contract was also responsible for confusing the role of the community organizer, and contributed to the defunding of the Coalition. For example, a CETA job title was Community Organizer, but people who held that position were not necessarily doing confrontational, power organizing, and did not need experience in community organizing as a condition for employment. Community organizers, under CETA, were required to have a high school diploma or experience in community work. When community organizers were sought for the Coalition, there was not a clear understanding about the work involved. In addition, CETA employees were often involved in raising funds, in order to pay for the rent and utilities for their organization's storefront. The importance of raising money for staff salaries did not exist. This idea was presented for the first time by the Coalition in an attempt to deal with impending budget cuts. In the end the Coalition competed with all local CETA organizations for funding. Thus, the relationship between CETA and the Coalition which initially was a strength ends as a flaw as the Coalition matures and requests that its member groups contribute to its self sufficiency. These events will be discussed in greater detail in later chapters.

VISTA VOLUNTEERS

Workers from Volunteers in Service to America (VISTA), the domestic affiliate of the Peace Corp, also had an important presence and played a major role in the development of the Greenpoint-Williamsburg community. In the 1970's, VISTA volunteers accepted placements in Greenpoint-Williamsburg. They could be found working on community projects which focused on housing, issue and tenant organizing, and local economic development. Many volunteers were college educated and commencing their professional careers through VISTA. Like CETA employees, VISTA volunteers also participated in the Coalition and attended community wide events and meetings. They, too, could be counted on to "turn out" community residents and to flock to neighborhood actions.

The purpose of this chapter was to contextualize the development of a community coalition in Greenpoint-Williamsburg devoted to activism. The community's tradition of social activism combined with the existence of CETA run by community organizations, and local volunteerism set the stage for a community coalition. Residents were accustomed to voluntary participation in community organizations, and were, to a certain extent, experienced in political action. They discerned that they had to "fight" for services. This history, combined with the community work of CETA employees and the mission of VISTA, created the Greenpoint-Williamsburg Coalition of Community Organizations.

Notes

1 All names are pseudonyms.

2 I would like to note that another building which combined a day care center and a senior citizens center was also constructed on 59th Street and 12th Avenue in Brooklyn. The original sponsoring organization was the Congress of Italian American Organizations (CIAO). The senior center is viewed as an Italian center. The combination of these services may be the way in which they were accepted by Italian communities.

3 Baci ball is an Italian game. It involves throwing a ball and coming close to or hitting a smaller, golf size ball on the court. An Italian restaurant in New York City called Il Vagabondo has a baci ball court in the dining room.

4 The area called the northside refers to the names of streets which range from North 1st Street to North 15th Street.

5 Stopping traffic on the Brooklyn-Queens Expressway (BQE) was a strategy frequently used by activists in Greenpoint-Williamsburg. Accessibility to the BQE is easy for residents since it runs through the community and is elevated in one section. The BQE is selected as a target because the traffic jam caused by residents is likely to attract coverage by the news media.

6 These leaders came primarily from Greenpoint, Italian Williamsburg, and the Northside because these were the areas with which June was most familiar.

7 These job slots excluded administrative staff, such as site liaison.

8 Comp time refers to the practice where an employee is given time off for extra hours worked instead of being paid an overtime rate.

CHAPTER 4

THE HISTORY AND DEVELOPMENT OF THE GREENPOINT-WILLIAMSBURG COALITION OF COMMUNITY ORGANIZATIONS

The tradition of community activism and the existence of CETA organizations, their workers, and VISTA volunteers, laid the groundwork for the development of a community coalition. Piven and Cloward (1977) note that collective actions are typically a response to social conditions which eventually become institutionalized. GWCOCO, however, was formed for the purpose of collective actions. In other words, institutionalization took place prior to mobilization. The creation of the GWCOCO began with the formation of the Greenpoint-Williamsburg Organizing Project, which evolved into Neighbors of Greenpoint and Williamsburg. "Neighbors" acted as a sponsoring committee which gave birth at a founding convention to the Greenpoint-Williamsburg Coalition of Community Organizations. The Coalition developed in a way that was contrary to Piven and Cloward's (1977) thesis in that it did not develop as a result of insurgency. The organization was first formed and disruptive tactics were used to protest conditions.

This chapter will describe how the Coalition's development led to the creation of a representative body of community organizations who participated in a founding convention. A discussion of the Coalition's mission, structure, external funding, staff and leadership will also be done. Finally, an examination of the conflicts which surfaced within the organization at its early stage of development will also be presented.

The idea of creating a coalition of community organizations in Greenpoint-Williamsburg originated with June Price. She reports,

> I had been to coalition meetings in Baltimore and
> Washington and other places. I always thought that was such
> a wonderful model. You'd go to these big conventions and
> there would be hundreds of people coming in from Legion
> Posts and Girl Scouts. That to me seemed the best model of
> community control, having that kind of input and
> involvement. I didn't create [the model], I had seen it [and
> attempted to replicate it].

Others involved with planning the Coalition say that "it grew from June's ties." These "ties" refer to June's relationship with Father Nick, a Catholic priest who worked at St. Vincent de Paul Church in Williamsburg. They met while protesting the expansion of S&S Corrugated Corporation. He became important for the realization of a community coalition. In the formation of the GWCOCO, Father Nick was responsible for obtaining the organization's initial funding from the Campaign for Human Development of the U.S. Catholic Conference. The Campaign for Human Development (CHD) is the social justice arm of the Catholic Church. Not only is Father Nick credited with obtaining this funding, but in fact, CHD funds for the Greenpoint Williamsburg Organizing Project were channeled through the church where he worked.[1] Technical assistance for submitting a proposal was given by another organization funded by CHD located in Washington D.C. The local person who actually wrote the proposal to submit to CHD[2] had the feeling that the proposal wasn't very important. She said, "the deal was already made; we were up for it." In other words, Father Nick had already acted as broker and negotiated a contract for Greenpoint-Williamsburg.

CHD was very interested in funding this community coalition in Greenpoint-Williamsburg because it was a project that included different races, ethnic groups, ages, as well as social classes in that it combined a working class and a poor community. From the standpoint of CHD and those in the community inventing a coalition, the project would bring different groups together to focus on local problems, shared community interests, and attempt to bring about local changes.

GREENPOINT WILLIAMSBURG ORGANIZING PROJECT

As previously stated, this organization developed from the brainstorming efforts of June Price and CETA staff working at the National Congress of Neighborhood Women (NCNW), and Ethnic Neighborhood Action Center (ENACT). They created the Greenpoint Williamsburg Organizing Project (GWOP), which in 1976, applied for funding to the Campaign for Human Development and was granted $74,500.[3] The stated objectives of GWOP were:

> To create a coalition of community organizations which reflects the ethnic and racial diversity in the area...The coalition will be self-governing and eventually self-supporting. The coalition will aim at developing indigenous leadership, through dealing with issues in individual neighborhoods, strengthening individual groups, identifying common issues among groups, thereby crossing neighborhood lines. The ultimate function of the coalition will be to provide a mechanism whereby poor and working class people develop enough power so that they may bring about institutional change and that neighborhoods become an integral and viable part of the decision making process.[4]

GWOP did the preliminary work for what later became the Greenpoint-Williamsburg Coalition of Community Organizations. GWOP organized local leadership and community organizations in both Greenpoint and Williamsburg to be members of the Coalition.

The organizational structure of GWOP included two boards, a board of directors and a policy making board. The board of directors was comprised of five Catholic priests who were responsible for the administration of funds. As previously stated, a grant from CHD was channeled through a local Catholic church to GWOP. The policy making board was made up of eleven lay community leaders. They were responsible for planning the organization's agenda. The intention was that "the two boards will function in a mutually exclusive manner. The board of directors will merely allocate monies to those projects presented by a consensus of the policy making board."[5]

A member of the policy making board reported that clergy comprised the board of directors because CHD suggested it. This respondent said, "That's how we started. The way to get to people was through the clergy. Churches had many societies." This suggests that from the initial stages of development, it was certain that churches would be recruited as part of this organizing effort. Local churches gave GWOP the opportunity to reach thousands of community residents. Another respondent explained,

> The model of this Coalition includes church based support...I understood from an organizing perspective what the Catholic Church could do. I would meet these priests from the Southside in the Hispanic community who were wonderful. I thought, why are these priests from the white ethnic community and the Hispanic community not working together. They're Catholics!

This respondent obviously recognized the potential of the local Catholic Church in organizing their congregations around community issues.

This organizational structure of GWOP was expected to be temporary. As community organizations were recruited as members, they would eventually elect a governing board and GWOP's original structure would dissolve. GWOP proposed the following:

> The organizers will talk and meet with leaders, residents, and local groups...As community leaders emerge, existing groups become strengthened and new groups form, the creation of the coalition will begin. We anticipate that the organizing effort will continue for nine to twelve months. At the end of this first phase, we expect to hold a community convention. The convention will provide an opportunity for delegates from participating organizations to meet to name the coalition, adopt a constitution, draw up by-laws, elect officers, vote on issues and agree on priority rank of those issues to be acted upon.[6]

In this way, a coalition would develop through its local organizations as a democratic body reflecting the racial, ethnic, and economic diversity of the community. While the organization was going through the process of legal incorporation, it changed its name to Neighbors of Greenpoint and Williamsburg.

NEIGHBORS OF GREENPOINT and WILLIAMSBURG

The organization opened a storefront on Metropolitan Avenue, in the Italian section (Central Williamsburg), and the geographical center of Greenpoint-Williamsburg. "Neighbors" started its work with a staff comprised of an executive director (a position filled by the person who wrote and submitted the grant proposal to CHD), two full-time community organizers, four part-time community organizers, and a full-time secretary. A consultant/trainer was retained to meet with staff and review their approach to issues and organizing techniques. One of the full-time organizers was a young, black man. Until then, there had not been a history of hiring blacks for community work, especially in Greenpoint and the Italian section of Williamsburg. In order to create a coalition which would reflect the cultural diversity of the community, however, the sponsoring committee placed a priority on hiring an integrated organizing staff. This organizer recalled his interview,

> I walk into the place. There were [a number of people from the board of directors and policy making board] there. Nobody was black! I thought, "this is ridiculous. I'm not going to be hired"...As I'm leaving they said, "we'll call you in a few days." I thought, "forget it." [The director] called me in a couple of days and hired me.

This man was actually the most experienced of the staff members. He had worked as a community organizer, and had been involved in a number of civil rights groups in Harlem, including the Civil Rights Movement, Congress for Racial Equality (CORE), and National Association for the Advancement of Colored People (NAACP). He later terminated his employment in Greenpoint-Williamsburg, and went to work for the Industrial Areas Foundation (IAF), a national organizing network founded by the late Saul Alinsky.

Neighbors of Greenpoint and Williamsburg accomplished a number of tasks in the community. It established several block associations and tenants organizations. In East Williamsburg, the staff of Neighbors assisted in the development of a civic council, "which has a membership of 13 groups comprising 147 residents."[7] The organization also monitored and collected data in conjunction with another organization, the St. Nicholas Neighborhood Preservation and Housing Rehabilitation Corporation, on redlining in the community. These two groups sponsored a local committee on redlining, and gave presentations to community groups. Further, the staff of "Neighbors" attended a demonstration on redlining at the Waldorf Astoria, while a bankers meeting was being held inside the hotel. Neighbors of Greenpoint and Williamsburg also reapplied for a second year of funding from CHD.

The activity carried out by the staff of "Neighbors," which was probably the most important one in terms of the organization's future, was the recruitment of community organizations as member groups of an emerging GWCOCO. The organizing staff of "Neighbors" met with the membership of local organizations in Greenpoint and Williamsburg explained their mission and the need to create a community coalition. As an additional incentive, the staff of Neighbors provided technical assistance and resources to local organizations. Initially, this was how member organizations were recruited. According to one staff member, "we befriended them and helped them with their causes and issues. We gave them what counted with them."

THE FOUNDING CONVENTION

On November 20, 1977, the policy board of Neighbors sponsored the first annual convention to introduce a coalition of neighborhood groups. This convention was made possible

> Through a planning process that established 5 committees of committed neighborhood leaders. The committees were: arrangements, constitution, membership/credentials, resolutions, and nominations...Each committee reported to seven open, public pre-convention meetings held throughout the community. Input was elicited and incorporated into the committee meetings. Each committee was open until the convention date.[8]

Roughly 99 community organizations attended the convention. They were represented by approximately 575 delegates.[9] At the convention, delegates ratified a constitution, enacted resolutions to be achieved by this coalition during the coming year, and elected officers. Twenty-two people were elected to the following positions: 4 executive members, which included the president, executive vice president, secretary, treasurer, and 3 area vice presidents from each of the 6 ethnic enclaves in Greenpoint-Williamsburg identified by the sponsoring committee. The 22 member board included: 3 Poles, 6 Italians, 7 Hispanics, 4 African

Americans, and 2 Irish. Of these, 12 were women and 10 were men. They were leaders from senior centers, federations of block associations, tenants groups, youth groups, human service centers, ethnic leagues, and housing development agencies. The major event at this convention was the founding of the Greenpoint-Williamsburg Coalition of Community Organizations (GWCOCO).

Around the same time, Neighbors of Greenpoint and Williamsburg was awarded another grant for $75,000 from CHD. This second grant covered the period of December 1, 1977 to November 31, 1978. An agreement was made between Neighbors of Greenpoint and Williamsburg and the Greenpoint-Williamsburg Coalition of Community Organizations, which included the following terms:

> Neighbors of Greenpoint and Williamsburg will place the $75,000 grant at the disposal of the Coalition if Neighbors is assured that the Coalition will honor the budget agreement with the Campaign for Human Development.[10]

The staff of Neighbors was transferred to the Coalition. The board of Neighbors met quarterly with the Coalition in order to oversee the expenditure of funds awarded by CHD for a second year, but this was the sole relationship that existed between Neighbors and GWCOCO. The newly elected board members of GWCOCO were responsible for planning, and policy. Eventually, the Coalition was incorporated as a not-for-profit, tax exempt organization (501c3), and Neighbors of Greenpoint and Williamsburg was dissolved as a corporation.

GREENPOINT-WILLIAMSBURG COALITION OF COMMUNITY ORGANIZATIONS

The founding convention gave the Coalition's staff an agenda of issues for the subsequent year. Delegates expressed major concern over increasing crime and redlining. Delegates wanted the Coalition to continue negotiating agreements with banks, a stage toward fair lending practices. Thirdly, delegates wanted action taken against a local movie theater which exhibited pornographic films and live burlesque. In addition, the problem of poor sewers, which overflowed and caused flooding in the basements of residents' homes, was identified as a problem requiring immediate attention. Finally, the need for external funding and internal fund raising operations were ongoing themes. The staff and board gave importance to identifying new sources of funding. Soon after the founding convention, the Coalition developed and submitted a grant proposal to the Law Enforcement Assistance Administration (LEAA) of the United States Justice Department. The narrative focused on community crime prevention in which block and civic associations would be formed or reactivated to involve more residents in community affairs. The proposal was designed so that each geographic area of the Coalition would be supplied with its own community organizer.

The original, elected leaders of the Coalition were unsure of this coalition's direction. In fact, many got themselves elected because they knew "something was happening," and they not only wanted to be a part of it, but did not want to miss a potential opportunity. The Coalition's first president was closely aligned with Father Nick, the Catholic priest who was influential in obtaining CHD funds for the original organizing project. She was a resident of Italian Williamsburg and was elected because "the Italians had the most people [at the Convention]." Many of the elected board members saw the Coalition as a vehicle to acquire personal power within the community, and to protect their own ethnic niche or fiefdom. Some had political aspirations and saw this coalition as a way to launch a career in local electoral politics. Others wanted to develop relationships that could lead to employment in City government. Thus, in the early years, people were involved because they were motivated by self-interest. According to one of the organizers,

> It was self-interest we were really using. In other words, if you don't come in the whites are going to get it. If you don't come in the blacks are going to get it. If you don't join somebody else is going to take it. And if you want your piece of the action you better be a part of it.

Ethnic and racial differences were used effectively to recruit member organizations. With this approach, people wanted to be involved in the Coalition. They did not want their people left out of the process or the Coalition's future activities.

The Coalition's staff and leaders spent their first year getting settled in a new office, which was located on the second floor of 1129 Catherine Street, the former site of St. Nicholas High School. They also became acquainted with new leadership, and continued to recruit member organizations. The new president believed that Father Nick, the priest who advocated for her

> Saw me as a safe leader who would bring the Coalition back
> on track and more appropriate for CHD than the more radical
> direction of the board and staff.

A schism developed within the organization between church based leaders and community activists over who would control the Coalition and by extension, whose ideology would direct the organization. The election of this "safe" president was an attempt by a member of the clergy to take charge.

This president was concerned about the way in which the Coalition was expending CHD's funds which was probably a contention of Father Nick. At the organization's first delegate assembly meeting[11], which was held on January 11, 1977, shortly after the founding convention, the president's primary focus was on an expensive phone system which was rented by the staff. One delegate recalled,

> The first assembly everybody gets together. They're about to
> push an issues package. [The president] starts questioning the
> phone system that was installed, and they had an hour
> conversation about the phone system.

Some staff members felt that the president did not agree with the activists' view that the purpose of the Coalition was an issue/action oriented organization. Church based leaders believed this approach was too radical. Obviously, these different definitions of the Coalition's role among the original leadership confused the objectives and agenda for its first delegate assembly meeting. The organization's constitution, however, viewed the delegate assembly as the policy and decision making body of the Coalition. Along with the discussion of the phone system, one order of business that was authorized at the first delegate assembly was the creation of a committee to plan a community wide youth olympics. After approximately four months, the president of the Coalition accepted a position with New York City's government and resigned. Although her letter of resignation stated that she was disturbed over a possible conflict of interest with her new job, she was actually concerned that the Coalition would embarrass her by the tactics used, such as stopping traffic on New York City's highways, and marching on City Hall. Several other resignations were submitted as well over the first few months. They came from officers who were not willing to embrace an issue/social action oriented organization. These difficulties experienced by the Coalition were resolved during its first six months of existence. The events responsible for solving these problems were: the resignation of the first president, the election of a new president who advocated social action, and a positive experience from the Youth Olympics, which will be discussed shortly and in more detail in Chapter 5.

DECISION MAKING AND CONTROL

The first six months of the Coalition's existence was fraught with confusion over roles and jobs. Shortly after their election, the Coalition's board asserted its control. Patterns of staffing changed somewhat. For example, two part-time organizing positions were converted into a full-time position, two CETA workers from Catholic Charities were stationed at the Coalition, and two VISTA workers were secured. In addition, a graduate student in urban planning from Hunter College of the City University of New York used the Coalition as a field placement.

From the outset, the leadership made virtually all decisions, including: the hiring of staff, retention of a consultant's services, and submission of grant proposals to foundations and government funding sources. The following excerpts were extrapolated from the minutes of board meetings, illustrating this claim.

> [A board member] moved that no action on the hiring of CETA personnel be taken until the next Executive Committee meeting of February 28th unless it is absolutely necessary to hire before then, in which case a special meeting of the Executive Committee will be held.[12]

The Executive Officers agreed that in light of the present financial difficulties   of the Coalition, [the consultant\ staff trainer's] services would not be retained at the present time, but that the Coalition might need his services again on an   as-needed basis. [A member] added that the Executive Officers, not the   executive   director,   would   have   the authority to determine if and when such an occasion would arise in the future.[13]

> [A board member] made a motion that the Coalition Finance

> Committee be involved with the Executive Officers in all
> proposal writing matters, that abstracts of a proposal be
> submitted to the Executive Committee members before the
> proposal itself is submitted and that any proposals over a
> certain amount of money be submitted to the Executive
> Committee at a special meeting for their prior consideration
> and approval...[and] all proposals to foundations should be
> cleared by the Coalition Finance Committee in advance.[14]

All of these motions were passed unanimously. The organizational dilemma created by board control was that the staff were more knowledgeable and had far more expertise in these matters than the leadership. For example, many board members did not understand community organizing, yet they were hiring community organizers. Also, the board was not informed about the staff's developmental needs, but would decide without staff input whether or not to hire a consultant. This pattern of control by the board remained a characteristic of the Coalition. Leaders obtained a feeling of personal power from decision making, however, this practice hurt the organization overall because the staff, especially the executive director, had limited power to do what he/she thought was best for the organization. This was augmented by the fact that the board often failed to accept the Director's recommendations.

Since there was a lack of knowledge and training of the Coalition's board regarding social action, the elected leaders managed the Coalition in the same way that they ran CETA funded organizations. Furthermore, the presence of CETA contributed to a situation in which Coalition board members and leaders were also CETA employees or board members of CETA organizations. For most, of these leaders, administering an organization which contained CETA employees was their only experience. In addition, the Coalition's first executive director attempted to "manage the board" as opposed to train them. She was unable to make the transition from recruitment for the founding convention, that is convincing people to join the Coalition, to teaching the value of issue organizing and relationship building across racial lines. This void left the elected leaders in the position of assuming the only role of board member they grasped, which was that of hiring residents and friends and controlling employees and funds. The lack of an effective executive director displays itself in the fact that the Coalition's initial community organizing efforts were performed by the assistant director, not the executive director. This illustrates that the executive director was not a community organizer while the assistant director had experience in this

area, but more importantly it symbolically conveys to the elected leaders
that the importance of organizing was secondary. In May of 1978, a new
president was elected at a delegate assembly, and after consultation with
the new president, the executive director resigned during the summer of
1978. With her leaving the assistant director, who had the most
experience and training in community organizing, was promoted to
executive director. He worked with the board and staff to develop an
agenda of community issues for the organization. Both, the new
executive director and the new president viewed the resignation of the
previous executive director as positive for the Coalition's development.

FINANCIAL DIFFICULTIES

With a second year of funding from CHD, a founding convention,
and a new location, the Coalition faced funding problems. Specifically,
the organization was overspending its budget. As noted earlier,
Neighbors of Greenpoint and Williamsburg served as a channeling
agency for CHD funds to the Coalition, and the "Neighbors" board
oversaw the Coalition's expenditure of CHD money. In a letter to CHD,
the chairperson of "Neighbors" wrote,

> With the 1st quarterly report, we submitted a letter
> expressing our concerns regarding overspending by the
> Coalition and enumerating possible cost cutting measures.
> The Coalition has taken several concrete steps and followed
> the cost cutting suggestions outlined; Neighbors board
> applauds this effort. Although, local contributions as
> reflected in the report have been achieved, Neighbors board
> has noted that more of a fund raising effort is needed.[15]

The board of the Coalition was well aware of its financial situation and
discussed various remedies at monthly meetings. The minutes of one
meeting reflect the following exchange:

> [The treasurer] then requested [the assistant director] to
> provide the Executive Committee with a detailed report on
> the financial condition of the Coalition...[The assistant
> director] stressed that CHD funds should be used specifically
> for salaries, fringe benefits and insurance costs for the five
> CHD staff members and that these funds should not be used
> to pay rent, telephone expenses and gas bills.In order to pay

> the Coalition's expenses until the Second Convention, [the
> assistant director] advocated the following: (a) have a
> Coalition fund-raiser every month, (b) institute a membership
> fee for Coalition agencies (suggested fee: $2 per organization
> per month) (c) have the Coalition obtain a 501(c)(3) as
> quickly as possible and use the tax exempt status to get
> funding from various organizations on a top priority basis.[16]

The only recommendation that was acted on was the procurement of a
501c3, which gave the organization tax exempt status, and made it
eligible as a not for profit corporation to receive grants from private
foundations and government agencies. The monthly fund raiser never
occurred, although, an annual event was held, the Greenpoint-
Williamsburg Youth Olympics and Minithon, which came to serve as a
yearly fund raiser. This event was originally planned for the purpose of
recreation, and to encourage the growth of relationships which crossed
ethnic and racial borders. The Youth Olympics will be discussed in detail
in the next chapter. A membership fee or a schedule of dues paid to the
Coalition by its member groups was never instituted. In order to filter
more cash into the Coalition and instill more of a sense of ownership by
delegates, the assistant director (who is the same person who was
promoted to executive director) and a later executive director were very
much in favor of the member organizations contributing financially to
their coalition. The lack of a dues structure impaired the Coalition in the
end, when virtually all of its sources of income disappeared. This decline
will be discussed in a later chapter. By its second convention, however,
the Coalition had been reprieved from its financial troubles with a
$248,000 grant, over 18 months, from the Law Enforcement Assistance
Administration (LEAA), effective October 1978. These funds were
successfully acquired by the Coalition pressuring the local Congressman.
The organization's situation shifted from one of cost containment to
expansion, which included the hiring of additional staff. The organization
was also seeking support from private foundations. The Coalition's
financial success through LEAA eventually became its downfall since
this grant delayed the necessity of the organization reaching a level of
monetary self sufficiency and independence.

THE LEAA GRANT

The Coalition was funded to carry out a community based, anti-crime project. The ultimate goal was to curtail a rising crime rate. This program was implemented by actively involving residents of the community to participate in local organizations and events. The Coalition's community organizers spent time with their respective area vice presidents and other leaders, and assisted in the formation of block associations, merchant's groups, and civilian observation patrols, which then became members of the Coalition. They also linked interested individuals and organizations with the local police precinct's block watcher program. Moreover, the organizing staff researched the concerns of leaders in an attempt to learn who or what government agency was responsible for various problems, and then worked at having the problem corrected. For example, leaders would bring abandoned and unsealed buildings to the attention of the Coalition and staff would push the City bureaucracy to have these buildings sealed or demolished.

The Staff

Under the LEAA grant, the organizing staff of the Coalition increased dramatically. A project director was hired, as well as an organizer for each geographic/ethnic area of the community, which were represented in the Coalition by area vice presidents. A senior citizen and a youth organizer were also hired. As discussed earlier, the board of directors controlled hiring. With a considerable number of positions to fill, the hiring process became overtly political. Area vice presidents encouraged certain community residents, often friends and neighbors, to apply for positions, and the board ultimately hired these people. Often, agreements were made among these board members to support each other's candidate in the hiring process. In general, the board viewed staff positions as patronage jobs, as opposed to an opportunity to recruit experienced people. A board member's ability to hire a friend conveyed that he/she was powerful. The organization's first year, with its initial president and executive director, and the prior experience of elected leaders with CETA organizations, set the stage for these practices. Most of those hired, including the project director, did not have any experience as community organizers. Some came with community work experience, some had college degrees, and others had never before been employed on a full-time basis. Each organizer reflected the ethnicity of the portion of the community for which they were responsible. Organizers also represented the interests of the board member who advocated for them, and had them hired. A relationship based on loyalty ensued. Organizers were indebted to particular leaders for their jobs. Board members often hired friends and neighbors who they perceived would serve as their support staff. This power dynamic was arranged from the start. As one organizer described,

> I was an original staff person. I was only eighteen at the time. I got the job because of who I knew, not what I knew...Basically what I did was a lot of networking with the member agencies from that particular part of the district, and working with that leadership to prioritize their issues and to help move them.

The LEAA staff was given opportunities to develop organizing skills from the executive director. The staff members were also assisted by trainers from various schools of community organizing. Ultimately, however, the staff was loyal to the board member(s) who was responsible for hiring them. They were not faithful to the executive director and his plans. Obviously, this situation restricted the effectiveness of the executive and project directors in terms of supervision, staff accountability, and unity of purpose.

THE SECOND YEAR

By the second convention the organization was fiscally secure, and was on its way to developing a presence in the community. Its organizers were out in the community meeting with people, investigating problems, and working on issues. The new president, who was elected at a delegates' assembly in May, and made community issues the focus of these meetings, was re-elected at the second convention. This person was compatible with a social action approach. He believed in issue organizing and was clearly committed to the mission of the Coalition. He was a delegate from Greenpoint who chaired the board of directors of a local senior center, and had been the director of a neighborhood youth program. He also ran a successful youth olympics and mini-marathon for the Coalition, mentioned earlier, which involved member organizations throughout Greenpoint and Williamsburg. In fact, within the first year of the LEAA grant, the project director resigned inciting this president to leave his leadership office and apply for the staff position. His application was strongly supported by the executive director who had been functioning as his mentor. He was hired and remained an employee until

1980 when he was trained by the Industrial Areas Foundation and employed by one of their projects. With the direction of the executive director, who had organizing experience, and this new project director, who was eager to learn and to take on issues, the Coalition was on its way to developing into a powerful community organization.

Notes

[1] Greenpoint Williamsburg Organizing Project's Application for Funding, Campaign for Human Development.

2 This person was employed under CETA by National Congress of Neighborhood Women. She worked primarily as a tutor and taught classes to prepare people for an examination leading to a General Equivalency Diploma.

3 Grant Agreement between the United States Catholic Conference and the Greenpoint Williamsburg Organizing Project, p. 1.

4 Greenpoint Williamsburg Organizing Project's grant proposal submitted to the Campaign for Human Development, p.3.

5 Greenpoint Williamsburg Organizing Project's grant proposal submitted to the Campaign for Human Development, p.6.

6 Greenpoint Williamsburg Organizing Project's grant proposal submitted to Campaign for Human Development, p. 8-9.

7 Neighbors of Greenpoint and Williamsburg's Quarterly Progress Report submitted to the Campaign for Human Development. This report was for the 3rd quarter, which ranged from May 16, 1977 to August 15, 1977, p. 3.

8 Neighbors of Greenpoint and Williamsburg's Quarterly Progress Report submitted to the Campaign for Human Development. This report is for the 4th quarter, which ranged from August 16,1977 to November 15, 1977, p. 2.

9 Ibid., p. 2B.

10 Ibid., Attachment C.

11 Delegate assembly meetings were held every two months and included one representative from each member organization.

12 Minutes of an Executive Committee meeting held on Thursday, January 26, 1978.

13 Minutes of an Executive Committee meeting held on February 28, 1978.

14 Minutes from Executive Committee meetings held on February 28, 1978 and April 4, 1978.

15 Letter from the board of directors of Neighbors of Greenpoint and Williamsburg to the Campaign for Human Development dated May 16, 1978.

16 Minutes of the Executive Committee meeting held on Tuesday, April 4, 1978.

CHAPTER 5

THE ISSUES

The Coalition worked on a variety of local issues including additional traffic and street lights, adequate sewers, more police for public housing, the demolition of dangerous buildings, the maintenance of investment practices and essential city services. Issues were divided into two major groups: individual problems that each of the Coalition's geographic districts cited for resolution, and concerns that affected the whole Greenpoint-Williamsburg community. This chapter will describe some of the major issues the Coalition confronted. It will include both local area matters, as well as Coalition wide struggles. With the exception of the Youth Olympics and the formation of merchants' associations, in most cases the approach used was one of confrontational, community organizing.

The Coalition staff emulated the style of Saul Alinsky even though they had not been trained by the Industrial Areas Foundation (IAF). As one of the Coalition's organizers described,

> It was all Saul Alinsky style organizing, that's what we were doing. Our bible was <u>Rules for Radicals</u>. I think what ACT UP is doing today is very similar to that type of organizing. It's very aggressive, it's militant in a way, it's very attention

grabbing. We did a lot of stuff. We were good for our really
wild demonstrations, which grabbed the attention we were
looking for so that an issue could be hot. We did a mock car
accident. We had people all bloodied up laying all over the
streets. We blocked the BQE [Brooklyn-Queens
Expressway] during the height of rush hour a couple of
times. A few leaders were arrested for that one.

The Alinsky approach to organizing involves identifying a common
enemy, target, or threat and using it to bring people together across racial
and/or local geographic divisions. Once people focus on a common
enemy and are empowered by a unified action, they are motivated to
work together and build an organization (Alinsky 1971). This was the
Coalition's model.

Along with the issues, this chapter will also present strategies and
tactics developed and utilized by the staff in order to accomplish
successful outcomes.

INDIVIDUAL AREA ISSUES

The Italians Organize: The Richardson Street Traffic Light Battle

A block association in Central Williamsburg demanded a traffic light
on the corner of Lorimer and Richardson Streets.[1] Members of the
Lorimer-Richardson Block Association claimed to have witnessed
through the years numerous accidents at this intersection causing deaths
and injuries. The block association had made previous requests to New
York City's Traffic Department but decided this time that they would not
take "no" for an answer. Surveys of this corner by the Traffic
Department determined that there was not enough traffic to require a
light.[2] Assisted by the Coalition's organizers, this block association, along
with member support from the North Henry Street Block Association,
developed a strategy for action

> [They] went directly to Traffic Department headquarters in
> Long Island City and, to dramatize their point, presented a
> traffic accident 'victim' to the office of Deputy Commissioner
> Thomas Guthrie.[3]

The delegation confronted Guthrie with their demands. The "victim" was a resident who was bandaged and bloodied and made to resemble an accident victim. In addition, the Coalition alerted the press about this plan, and a local television station covered the action. Media coverage further encouraged the group. The result was that the Commissioner's office studied the corner, concluded that there was a problem, and repositioned stop signs to be more obvious to the eyes of drivers.

Merchants Organize on the Southside

The combined efforts of the Coalition and Los Sures, a housing organization and Coalition member on the southside of Williamsburg, resulted in the formation of an association of merchants whose stores are located along Broadway, Havemeyer, and Grand Streets.[4] This project was part of the Southside's plan for revitalization and economic development. The association's first project was to hang Christmas lights along this commercial strip of Williamsburg. Merchants contributed money and December 1980 was "the first time in 25 years holiday lights will be up and on."[5] The Coalition's organizer, who assisted in the formation of this merchants' association, believed that the Christmas lights "are a symbol of pride and give the neighborhood merchants incentive to stay and build the community."[6]

Public Housing Residents Battle Housing Authority in East Williamsburg

The Tenants Association of Hylan Houses in Williamsburg, was a member of the Coalition and in fact, the Association's president was also an area vice president of the Coalition. Tenants were angry about their living conditions and New York City Housing Authority's neglect of the building and, by extension, the residents.[7] Assisted by the Coalition, a meeting was held between tenants and representatives of the Housing Authority. Sixty tenants presented a list of 15 complaints which required repairs or replacement of the following: elevator, intercom system, incinerator, mailboxes, pipes, lights, corridors, staircases, and the hot water system.[8] At the meeting, the Housing Authority concurred with the tenants' grievances and committed to completing work on their stated problems within nine months.[9] The Tenants Association promised to monitor the efforts and accomplishments of the Housing Authority.

Greenpointers Mobilize to Stop Truck Traffic

Like the traffic light issue in Central Williamsburg, the members of the Huron, Green, and India Streets Block Association complained of heavy trucks using residential blocks as quicker routes from local bridges and highways to Greenpoint's waterfront and commercial areas. This block association claimed that the trucks were causing water mains to break.[10] The association wanted "No Truck Traffic" signs posted, and made their request to New York City's Department of Transportation. The City carried out a study and found no problem with trucks in the area. This angered residents who were prepared to take more drastic action. With the assistance of the Coalition's organizers, members of the block association stopped traffic for an hour on McGuinness Boulevard, where it intersected with Huron, Green, and India Streets.[11] McGuinness Boulevard is a major traffic artery and links, by way of the Pulaski Bridge, the Queensborough Bridge (59th Street Bridge) and the Queens Midtown Tunnel with the Brooklyn-Queens Expressway. The delegation also made a surprise visit to Transportation Commissioner Ameruso's office. They carried signs which read, "No Trucks on Residential Streets," and "No Trucking on Side Streets."[12] This tactic worked, and "No Truck Traffic" signs were placed exactly where the block association wanted them.

It is important to note how the same strategies were often used for different issues or on different targets. Storming a commissioner's office was used by Huron, Green, India Streets Block Association to obtain "No Truck Traffic" signs for their blocks, as well as by the Lorimer-Richardson Street Block Association to secure a traffic light. Further, in an attempt to have an abandoned factory demolished, residents charged City Hall, an action that will be discussed later.

Local Resident Patrols Created with Coalition Support

Civilian patrols are a voluntary crime prevention program which involve residents. In Greenpoint-Williamsburg, block and tenant associations developed patrols for their immediate area or building. The first patrol in the community emerged from a block association in Greenpoint in response to automobile thefts and vandalism. Civilian patrols operate as a system in which two residents drive in one car and monitor the street activity of a specific segment of the neighborhood, usually the area where members live. Cars are equipped with CB radios.

If they encounter a suspicious event, they use the radio and inform the person listening at the base or other end of the radio. The base operator responds by calling the police. Those on patrol do not become directly involved in neighborhood disturbances. When residents from other member groups of the Coalition expressed concern over increasing crime, the functioning patrols offered them aid and training to start their own patrol. This assistance allowed patrols to develop throughout Greenpoint-Williamsburg. Residents were further encouraged by the captain of the 94th police precinct when he stated at a community meeting that "since the newly formed Civilian Patrol began in his area, burglaries have decreased in the area patrolled by 80%."[13] The patrols also served as a regular source of information to the Coalition and the community about police and crime activity. Furthermore, patrols allowed the Coalition to satisfy some requirements of the LEAA grant and to enhance their ability to be refunded for this anti-crime, organizing project.

Abandoned Meat Factory Meets the Mayor: The Trunz Campaign

A large factory owned by the Trunz Meat Corporation was situated on a lot bordered by Meeker,[14] Morgan and Kingsland Avenues and Lombardy Street. In 1972,[15] the business failed and the factory was abandoned. Over time the building deteriorated. The roof collapsed, windows were broken and unsealed, and an entrance was open.[16] The building was a hazard and threatened the safety of residents living in the surrounding neighborhood. A local newspaper reported,

> The Greenpoint residents had already lived through a lot of problems created by the abandoned building. A few years ago two boys were sodomized in the building. Drug sales are reported to be a common occurrence around the rotting hulk, and those dealing the drugs are not alone at the site: rats and stray dogs call the place home and venture forth from it to disturb neighbors of the plant. Numerous fires have also struck the old factory.[17]

The community had made several unsuccessful attempts to have the building demolished.

A number of member organizations of the Coalition decided to undertake this issue once again. The groups involved included: Neighborhood Facilities Corp., Italian American Multi Service Center, Morgan Avenue Block Association, Kingsland Avenue-Herbert Street

Area Block Association, North Henry Street Block Association, and the
94th Precinct Federation of Block Associations. This matter brought
together residents from Greenpoint and Central Williamsburg, since the
abandoned factory was situated on the border of these two areas. On
April 18, 1979, concerned residents met and established "a committee to
Demolish the Trunz Building."[18] This committee was assisted by
community organizers from the Coalition. The first step taken by the
committee was to submit of a list of demands to the New York City
Department of Housing Preservation and Development (HPD). The
committee insisted that HPD take the following action:

> 1. Agree to have the Trunz Building declared an "Unsafe
>   Building" within 30 days.
> 2. Agree to have the building exterminated for rodents.
> 3. Agree in writing to this committee that the building will be
>   scheduled for demolition within 90 days.
> 4. Agree to fence the property after demolition is
>   completed.[19]

One week later the local state senator arranged a meeting with the
community and city officials. Representatives from New York City's
Department of Buildings and Public Development Corporation attended,
but the person responsible for demolitions was noticeably absent.[20] At
this meeting the community learned that finances were influencing the
City's decision. A local newspaper reported the following:

> At the heart of the problem is money. The building was
> assessed by the city at $439,000, and there are back taxes
> owed on it to the tune of some $800,000, the meeting was
> told. In addition, it would cost the city a large sum -
> variously estimated at between $125,000 and twice that
> amount - to take the old building down. The city is trying to
> minimize its own costs and maximize the return it hopes to
> get.[21]

The overall preference from the City's point of view was to place the
burden demolition or rehabilitation on another party. The best possibility
for the City was to sell the property, collect back taxes, and furnish the
new owner with the community's demands. The community, however,
was unwilling to wait any longer for the City to realize this best case.

By the end of the week, after this meeting with city officials, residents held a demonstration in front of the factory. "They marched into the intersection of Morgan and Meeker Avenues, bearing signs that read "Take It Down," and "Koch Don't Botch This One."[22] The committee planned another more striking demonstration including City Hall as a site and, therefore, obtain the attention of city-wide media. This one was held on May 11, 1979.[23]

"A People's Demolition," equipped with sledgehammers and hard hats attracted three television stations. The action started at the factory with residents, some of whom were senior citizens swinging sledgehammers, removing bricks from the building. These bricks were placed in a pick-up-truck, which was driven to City Hall by the local state senator. Once at City Hall, residents delivered the bricks to Mayor Koch, some gift-wrapped, as a Mother's Day gift. Participants were thrilled by the demonstration and excited by the television coverage. They later watched themselves on the evening news which featured for this story an elderly, Italian man swinging his sledgehammer at the abandoned building.

Behind the scenes, the local state senator and state assemblyman were fighting. The state senator sponsored meetings on this issue and participated in the actions, but he was also competing with other local politicians, the Coalition and the community residents for "kudos," the spotlight and glory. He wanted to be viewed as the "savior." Every photograph that appeared in newspapers about the Trunz Committee, or their demonstrations included the state senator. The state assemblyman also wanted credit for successfully handling the issue. In contrast to the state senator, he used his influence with the Mayor's office, worked with the Coalition, and did not monopolize the efforts of the Coalition and residents, or the media. The Coalition's organizers were aware of the conflict which existed between these politicians, and used these competing elites and their antagonistic relationship to advance the issue. The political battle intensified at a community meeting held by the state senator, where the state assemblyman's aide telephoned the meeting to speak to the Coalition staff person responsible for the Trunz issue. The aide asked the organizer if the Coalition would like to meet with the Mayor's office about Trunz. The local politicians believed that the Coalition's executive director aspired to public office and were concerned about having him as a rival, since he was also a resident of Greenpoint and could rally support. The organizer thought that such a meeting would benefit the community and scheduled the meeting unbeknownst to the senator. Again, this telephone conversation is taking place at a meeting chaired by the state senator. Subsequent to the call, the state senator states that he is unable to obtain a meeting with City officials making decisions about demolitions. The Coalition's organizer then raised his hand and said, "Excuse me Senator, the Greenpoint-Williamsburg Coalition has a meeting with the Mayor's office." Those in attendance, including the state senator, were stunned and broke into discussion. The Coalition's organizer was successful at disrupting the state senator's meeting and asserting the Coalition's ability to get things done. The organizer seized the opportunity to manipulate the state senator in the same way that the senator had exploited the Coalition.

The assemblyman was successful in obtaining a meeting for the Coalition with John LoCicero, Special Assistant to the Mayor. The assemblyman told the Coalition's staff that this meeting was intended for the Coalition's leaders who were on the committee to get the building demolished, the organizers working with the committee, and the assemblyman. The meeting was not to include the state senator.

The meeting with LoCicero was held the week after the demonstration at City Hall.[24] The state senator invited himself and could not be dodged. In addition to the senator's trouble with the assemblyman, Mayor Koch loathed this man. Thus, his presence was problematic. At the point that LoCicero was ready to see the community's 40 representatives, and the group was called into a meeting room at City Hall, the Coalition's executive director prevented the state senator from entering the meeting. The executive director kept this politician in the hall as the meeting progressed. Inside, LoCicero verbally agreed to the committee's demands, and sent a letter to the committee conceding to their requests. A newspaper account reported that the letter also stated that

> Bids [for demolition] would be sent out on June 1st ...in addition, the Buildings Department will seal up the structure on that day. The city hopes, LoCicero told concerned Greenpointers, to have it under the hammer within three months.[25]

By the Coalition's third convention, the abandoned Trunz factory was gone and the empty lot had been fenced. Today, this space is occupied by a wholesale, food outlet.

COALITION WIDE ISSUES

Unfair Lending Practices

One of the first issues addressed by the Coalition was redlining. It was quite common during the 1970's for banks to disinvest in inner city neighborhoods by refusing to offer mortgages, business, and home improvement loans. Segments of Greenpoint and Williamsburg were redlined by the major savings banks in the area, particularly Anchor Savings, The Dime Savings Bank, Green Point Savings Bank, Lincoln Savings Bank, Williamsburgh Savings Bank. The Greenpoint/ Williamsburg Committee Against Redlining (GWCAR) was formed on August 15, 1977 after data on redlining were presented at a Town Hall meeting. GWCAR was made up of staff and community leaders from a number of local groups including, the Pratt Center, Catholic Charities, Los Sures, St. Nicholas Neighborhood Preservation and Housing Rehabilitation Corp., People's Firehouse, and Neighbors of Greenpoint and Williamsburg.[26] A member of GWCAR described,

> People came to St. Nick's saying they couldn't get mortgages. The group investigated where the banks invested. Banks like Anchor were investing outside the community. [GWCAR] met with CEO's and brought people with them who were denied mortgages.

This committee was established prior to the Coalition's founding convention. An organizer employed by Neighbors of Greenpoint and Williamsburg, who later became the executive director of the Coalition, was a member of GWCAR and gave the group his organizing expertise. After the founding convention, the Coalition considered GWCAR a committee of the Coalition. GWCAR demonstrated in and around banks, and met with bank officials to press for changes in the banks' lending policies in the community. GWCAR wanted banks

> To continue taking ads for mortgage and home improvement loans; to consider each property for which a loan request is made separately and on the basis of the soundness of the building itself rather than in the context of the block it is on, which may include industry or run down buildings; to promise to use a percentage of the local deposits locally; to drop the restriction on loans going only to depositors in order

to encourage more activity; and to make an agreement on the banks' policies in writing.[27]

One demonstration took place on October 30, 1978 and

Saw about 45 anti-redlining protestors in [Halloween] masks enter the Broadway branch of the Williamsburgh Savings Bank, where they engaged in a discussion of bank policy with bank Vice President Jay Jones...The protest began on the steps of the building at about 6:00; about 15 minutes later, the anti-redliners went inside, where they gave out balloons and skeletons with anti-redlining slogans.[28]

Shortly after this action, GWCAR met with Jones to persuade him to sign an agreement outlawing anti-redlining practices. This is an example of the approach taken by GWCAR with banks in the community.

The Committee's breakthrough came when Anchor Savings committed $25 million "over the next 5 years in mortgage and home improvement loans,"[29] the largest pool of money to be invested in the community by a savings bank at the time. The Dime Savings Bank of Williamsburg pledged $1 million for local loans.[30] A similar agreement was obtained from Lincoln Savings Bank. According to the Coalition's executive director,

This was significant because it was probably the most successful redlining campaign in the country. What was unique about these fights was we got the CEO's to meet with us, and a lot of the redlining fights of that period did not get the CEO's at the table.

He further explained that Anchor Savings was trying to open another branch and GWCAR and the Coalition's demonstrations were holding it up. "That was the trigger that got Anchor to buy in." The other banks then followed Anchor's lead and committed to investing money in the community.

Anti-redlining efforts in the 1970's have resulted in additional positive outcomes for Greenpoint-Williamsburg which continue to exist in the 1990's. These are in the form of a Building Survival Program and a neighborhood credit union. A leader of the Coalition explained,

Redlining has resulted in the Building Survival Program.

Banks wouldn't give loans to people in city owned buildings that were abandoned. We still meet and give loans to people who need money to stay in their homes until they can get a 7A administrator. We give money for plumbing, roofs, boilers. It's a revolving loan fund, interest free. You must be in buildings managed by Los Sures, St. Nicholas, People's Firehouse. Another offshoot of redlining is the North Brooklyn Federal Credit Union. It still exists with $200 million. We give money to people who can not get it at a bank.

Other long term effects of the Coalition's efforts will be discussed in subsequent chapters.

Greenpoint-Williamsburg Olympics and Mini-Marathon Created by Coalition

There were also local events sponsored by the Coalition, which were community wide, and were organized to bring people of different races and cultures together in the spirit of unity. The Coalition's intention by these events was to begin to break down racial barriers among residents of Greenpoint-Williamsburg. One such event was the Youth Olympics.

On May 21, 1978 the Coalition sponsored the first annual Youth Olympics, which was held in McCarren Park. The Olympics had a number of purposes. One was to bring together the communities of Greenpoint and Williamsburg in a positive way so that the Coalition could continue to carry out its goal of uniting diverse ethnic groups. Another purpose of the Youth Olympics was to hold an event for community youth. A third reason for sponsoring a Youth Olympics was to introduce the Coalition to a larger group of residents. In a program distributed to those attending the Olympics was the following statement:

The Youth Olympics Committee of the Greenpoint-Williamsburg Coalition of Community Organizations proudly welcomes you to the First Annual Greenpoint-Williamsburg Youth Olympics and Minithon. Run in the Minithon, participate in the Olympics, listen to the bands, eat, drink and enjoy being with your friends and neighbors! But while you are having fun, remember the other reasons why this event was put together...For at least thirty years, people in Greenpoint-Williamsburg have been coming to realize more and more that if our beautiful community and its

way of life are going to be preserved, they are going to have
to band together on common issues and to work together for
common goals...If Greenpoint-Williamsburg is to stay
together at a time when so many other communities are
falling apart, we ourselves are going to have to do the work
of preservation...Last November many community groups
came together to found the Greenpoint-Williamsburg
Coalition of Community Organizations. The Coalition exists
to improve the quality of life for every man, woman and
child in northern Brooklyn and works to help all community
groups in their fight for political, social and economic justice
for Greenpoint-Williamsburg. In the Coalition all of these
community groups have a framework within which they can
meet one another, exchange ideas and information, make
contacts and strengthen their sense of community, which will
carry us all through the difficult times ahead. Many
community people do not know about the Greenpoint-
Williamsburg Coalition and one of the reasons behind
today's events is to introduce it to you. Coalition staff are
here to give you information and to answer your questions.
Talk to them and learn about your Coalition.[31]

The Olympics served as a public relations event, a recruitment drive, and
a fund raiser for the Coalition, as well as an attempt to get people from
adjacent communities talking and eventually working together.

The notion of uniting people of different ethnic groups and races by
this event was further illustrated by a group of students from Hunter
College of the City University of New York. A member of the Olympics
Committee, who was a film major at Hunter College, organized a student
film crew to record the day's events. They titled this film The BQE is
Closed. The symbolic meaning behind this title was that the Brooklyn-
Queens Expressway separated the neighborhoods of Greenpoint and
Williamsburg. On the day of the Coalition's Youth Olympics, however,
the BQE was closed suggesting that no divisions existed.

The day's events included: a six mile run through each of the 6 areas
of the community, boys and girls 50, 100, 220, 440, and 880 yard dashes,
and live music by local bands and musicians who volunteered to perform.
Youth participants were organized through local youth programs, sports
teams, block and tenants associations and schools. The event proved to be
successful to the goals of the Coalition and as an event by itself. People
were brought together and expressed their willingness to work with each
other on community issues, and the Youth Olympics was held for the

next four years. Each year it grew in attendance, in number of sports events, and even added an ethnic food festival.

St. Valentine's Day Massacre

Near Valentine's Day 1979, cuts in city services incited the Coalition's organizers to draw an analogy between the 1929 massacre in Chicago and the reduction of services in Greenpoint-Williamsburg.[32] It was one of the first major meetings addressing community wide issues held by the Coalition. Commissioners of five City agencies, including the Departments of Aging, Education, Employment, Parks, and Transportation were invited to this meeting which was attended by 150 residents.[33] Organizers used a giant score card to rate the bureaucrats' remarks to the community's demands. Those City officials who agreed to work with the Coalition scored a Valentine's heart, and those who refused to make a commitment to the organization achieved a noose. This was a successful strategy. Residents, and the Coalition's leadership began to comprehend the role and tactics of community organizers and the organization's potential for power and recognition. These City agencies either agreed to specific items that the Coalition raised, or conceded to a future meeting with the Coalition's leaders and staff to review problems. For example, "the Parks Department promised to produce a schedule for maintenance work on all the parks in [Greenpoint and Williamsburg],"[34] while the Board of Education committed to meet with the organization at a later date. At the meeting, the Department of Employment's commissioner agreed to provide 50 jobs for local youth. Departments of Transportation and Aging pledged to meet with the Coalition within six weeks.[35] The relationships that developed with City officials and agencies as a result of this action aided the Coalition on future issues. In some cases the Coalition established an ongoing, working relationship thereby having access to decision makers.

Residents Demand Seats in New High School

In 1979, New York City's Board of Education announced that the construction of Northeast Brooklyn High School was near completion. The Coalition was attentive to Board of Education projects because the Board did not always act on behalf of the community. One of the Coalition's leaders described,

> The high school issue, two things went on. One was that the
> project had stopped in terms of construction. Eastern District
> High School was always a dumping ground for Greenpoint-
> Williamsburg students who had no place else to go. That's
> where you went. But then they built a school they never
> completed and stopped funding. The community had to fight
> to get it started again. When it was completed, the
> community was zoned out.

Parents in Greenpoint-Williamsburg looked forward to sending their
children to a newly constructed school. However, the Board of Education
had drawn the school's zone in such a way that "almost a third"[36] of the
students in Greenpoint-Williamsburg were not eligible to attend the new
school. Students living east of Kingsland and Bushwick Avenues were
"zoned out," which included parts of Greenpoint, Central Williamsburg
(including Cooper Park and the St. Nick's area) and East Williamsburg. A
student "will not be able to attend the new school, even though he will
see it every morning from his kitchen window."[37] A committee of the
Coalition was formed to address this issue, and a series of community
meetings were held. The sentiment expressed at these meetings was that
residents wanted all students living in Community Board 1 to have access
to the school. On March 26, 1980, the Coalition held a public meeting
with officials of the Board of Education. At this meeting, the Board of
Education agreed to admit all youths living in Community Board 1. In
discussions which followed, the Board of Education guaranteed that "all
community youths could transfer to the new school as well."[38] A major
reason for the Board's responsiveness to the community was probably
because of the working relationship that developed from the St.
Valentine's Day Massacre.

Community Unites to Save Police Precinct

On June 4,1980, an article appeared in the New York Post entitled,
"City Hall Mulls Plan to Shut 14 Police Stations." Residents were
concerned by this article because although it did not cite particular
precincts, Greenpoint's 94th Precinct was going to be moved temporarily
while the building was rehabilitated. Leaders of the Coalition were
suspicious about the City's "real" plans for the 94th Precinct and
wondered if it was on Koch's "hit list." Their reasoning was plausible
since New York City is divided into smaller geographic districts called
community boards, and according to the New York City Charter, which

is New York City's constitution, the provision of services or service districts must be co-terminous with the boundaries of the Community Board. The 94th Precinct was not the only police precinct in the Community Board. One police precinct in the Community Board was, therefore, legal. The Coalition's leaders assembled to plan a strategy to fight the City. On July 17, a rally was held in front of the precinct house on Meserole Avenue "to let the Mayor know that he is not going to close down our police precinct."[39] One leader explained,

> It worked with the 94th Precinct. We had that big rally, everyone came out. We told each organization to send at least four people. We had some crowd. They [Koch's administration] said they would renovate and we figured they would close it. They would take the police out and say they were renovating and disappear. That was a time in the 70's when they were closing clinics, hospitals. That's what the City was doing.

The Coalition then invited Mayor Koch to address this issue at a community meeting on July 30. The Mayor declined, but sent an aide who was confronted by about 400 delegates. These residents had 2,000 signed pledges from their neighbors, which were collected by dozens of organizations, stating that they would physically occupy the police precinct should the City attempt to close it. Leader after leader rose at the meeting announcing the name of the organization he/she represented and the number of people who pledged to fight the City and occupy the police building should it close the 94th police precinct. Each leader then came forward and piled the signed pledges in front of the Mayor's aide. He was literally buried in paper by the time the leaders were done. It should be reiterated that the community had a tradition of occupation. As was previously discussed, in the late 1970's a firehouse on the Northside, Engine Company 212, was slated to be closed. Organized by a group called People's Firehouse, residents occupied the firehouse for a year until the City agreed to keep it open. The next day, the Mayor's aide called to say that Koch wanted to meet with the Coalition's leaders. The Coalition agreed to a meeting with the Mayor, but negotiated the submission of a package of local issues to the Mayor prior to the meeting. These proposals, which included items of concern and problems throughout Greenpoint-Williamsburg, would serve as the framework for the meeting with the Mayor. The Coalition sent Koch a 21 page document which outlined demands on community issues. Koch agreed to work with the

Coalition on these issues, and to address a delegation at the Coalition's Fourth Annual Convention which was scheduled for November 16, 1980. The Mayor also committed to speak at the Convention about the future of the 94th Precinct. It should be noted that this was the only time that the Hasidic Jewish community actively participated in the Coalition. Delegates from the Hasidic community attended the Fourth Annual Convention because Mayor Koch was the keynote speaker. In his speech at the Convention the Mayor made no reference to the 94th Precinct. In fact, the 94th Precinct was conspicuously absent from his address. After a series of meetings and phone calls between the Coalition and the Mayor's Office, Koch informed the Coalition in a letter dated December 12, 1980 that he "has no plans to close the 94th Precinct."[40]

Prior to the convention, a number of City agencies responded to the Coalition's issues package. Streets were cleaned, buildings sealed, and information was provided about program opportunities that organizations and residents could secure. The Coalition's leaders and organizers believed that the 94th police precinct issue had succeeded in conveying to the Mayor's office that they would benefit most by dealing directly with the Coalition. This approach contradicted the way in which business is typically done in that an organization would work through a system of government which on a local level includes a community board and elected politicians. This shift in the way that City Hall did business with the local community, was related to their perception of the Coalition's power, that the Mayor's office realized with the delivery of bricks from the former Trunz factory, and by observing a large, determined constituency at the meeting on the police precinct.

MUTUAL SUPPORT

The Coalition built momentum with each successful action or resolution. In fact, as one organizer expressed, "It was prestigious to be elected to the Coalition's Board of Directors." Member groups also learned that there was power in numbers. In other words, the larger the group attending a meeting or action, the better the outcome. The different areas of the Coalition began to share their most precious resource, residents. An organizer stated,

> Each area developed its own needs, its own issues and
> presented them to the whole [Coalition]. And each area was
> supportive of the other, and that started to break down some

> of the [racial] barriers. People were coming into the white
> neighborhoods, and the whites were going into Hispanic and
> black neighborhoods. They were finally coming together
> collectively around things that they felt were for the
> neighborhood...The Southside would come to Greenpoint
> saying, "look, we need help, we need your numbers to come
> and support us." Greenpoint people would go to the
> Southside. Southside would come to Greenpoint. The
> Coalition was a forum where people could finally come
> together around stuff and start to break down some of those
> barriers...I think that the structure that we had kind of forced
> interaction. We made sure all [ethnic] groups were
> represented on the Board.

Although the organization's structure did force interaction at board
meetings and delegate assemblies, it did not require them to gather at
other times. However, a "rainbow coalition"[41] did evolve. In terms of
individual area issues it was mentioned previously that another block
association aided Lorimer-Richardson Block Association in its
demonstration on the Traffic Department. Furthermore, the operators of
the original civilian patrol in Greenpoint assisted in the formation of other
patrols throughout Greenpoint and Williamsburg. One of the Coalition's
organizers viewed the Trunz campaign as a milestone for the
organization,

> Because it was the first time that the blacks and Hispanics
> really came and stood with the whites on a major fight. That's
> why Trunz was such a major win.

On community wide issues integration occurred more naturally because
all groups were involved or affected by the matter and its outcome. But
as board members became leaders on community wide concerns,
organizers attempted to have most ethnic groups represented. For
example, board members who spoke at the rally on the 94th police
precinct included a white man and a black woman. Obviously, this was
planned in advance of the rally. As one looked at the crowd attending a
Coalition activity it was apparent that "a gorgeous mosaic"[42] was
flourishing in northern Brooklyn.

The Role of Politicians

   Local elected politicians could not be members of the Coalition's
board, and political organizations could not become members of the
Coalition. Yet, politicians typically connected themselves to Coalition
activities, and attempted to make an issue their own. The matter of Trunz,
discussed earlier, is an example. The Coalition was successful at using
conflict between politicians to advance the issue and benefit the
community. They attended Youth Olympics, community meetings
sponsored by the Coalition, and some even attended the Coalition's
annual Conventions as a delegate from a member organization. The
Coalition had grown into a powerful organization and the politicians
knew it, but did not necessarily like it. According to a Coalition board
member,

> The politicians had to come out and do something because
> we were kicking ass like crazy. They had to deal with us. All
> their newsletters were about the Coalition. We were number
> 1. They were using us like crazy.

Local politicians exploited the Coalition. They often jumped on the
proverbial bandwagon of community issues that the Coalition was
addressing. They also took credit for the Coalition's accomplishments.
They did this by publishing the success of an issue in their newsletter,
and mailing it to residents. Whenever possible, the Coalition's organizers
took advantage of the politicians desire to participate and made requests
of them. The logic here was that the politicians would always be lurking
around, so the Coalition may as well acquire from them whatever they
could. For example, politicians would be asked to obtain a meeting with
some official for the Coalition, or to support a grant proposal submitted
by the Coalition. For the most part, local politicians were obliging and
carried out requests made by the Coalition.
   The Coalition existed to create civic leaders and activists, not loyal
constituents for politicians. Community issues were used by the Coalition
to build an organization. Furthermore confrontation was the strategy
selected in order to gain public and media attention thereby feeling more
empowered. Politicians needed to be managed by the Coalition. As
leaders and delegates of the Coalition, citizens initiated agendas and
politicians frequently scrambled to keep abreast of the Coalition's
activities. The participation of elected officials was viewed by the

Coalition's leaders and organizers as validation of the organization's power.

Notes

[1] "Lorimer-Richardson Demands Traffic Light," North Brooklyn Mercury, July 20-27, 1979, p. 5.

[2] Ibid.

[3] Ibid., p.5.

[4] "Yule Lights on in Biz Section," New York Daily News, December 1, 1980.

[5] Ibid.

[6] Ibid.

[7] Joel Gallob, "Hylan Tenants Win!," North Brooklyn News, February 16-22, 1979, p.1.

[8] Ibid., p. 33.

[9] Ibid., p.33.

[10] "Truck Traffic Protested," Greenpoint Gazette, May 15, 1980.

[11] Ibid.

[12] Program of the Fourth Annual Convention of the Greenpoint-Williamsburg Coalition of Community Organizations, Sunday, May 16, 1980, p. 13.

[13] "Civilian Patrols: The Answer?," North Brooklyn Mercury, July 20-27, 1979, p.8.

[14] Meeker Avenue is the service road to the Brooklyn-Queens Expressway in Greenpoint-Williamsburg.

[15] Editorial, North Brooklyn News, May 4-10, 1979, p.4.

[16] "Trunz: City's $ vs. People's Safety?," North Brooklyn News, May 4-10, 1979, p.8.

[17] Ibid., p.8.

[18] "Community and Coalition Band Together To Demand Demolition Of Trunz Building," Greenpoint Gazette, April 24, 1979, p.1.

[19] Ibid., p.1.

[20] Joel Gallob, "People to City: Demolish Trunz! Community Groups, Pols Demand Action," North Brooklyn News, May 4-10, 1979, p. 1.

[21] " Trunz: City's $ vs. People's Safety?," North Brooklyn News, May 4-10, 1979, p. 8.

[22] Ibid., p.8.

[23] Joel Gallob, "Vow Trunz Vigilance, Weigh Supermkt. Option," North Brooklyn Mercury, May 25-June 1, 1979, p.16.

[24] Ibid., p. 16.

[25] Ibid., p. 16.

[26] "Housing Activists Sought Underlining Causes," in North Brooklyn News, February 16-22, 1979, p. 17.

[27] Mark Jagged, "GWCAR Trick-or-Treats Bank," North Brooklyn News, November 3-9, 1978 p. 15.

[28] Ibid.

[29] Quarterly report submitted by Neighbors of Greenpoint and Williamsburg to the Campaign for Human Development, May 16-August 15, 1977.

[30] Program of the Fourth Annual Convention of the Greenpoint-Williamsburg Coalition of Community Organizations, Sunday, November 16, 1980, p. 9.

[31] Program of the Greenpoint-Williamsburg Coalition of Community Organizations 1st Annual Olympics and Minithon, Sunday, May 21, 1978, p. 3-4.

[32] Pablo Alonso, "Coalition Wins Jobs, Parks," North Brooklyn News, February 23-March 1, 1979.

[33] Ibid.

[34] Ibid., p.1.

[35] Ibid.

[36] Greenline, March 15, 1980 p.1

[37] Ibid.

[38] Program of the Fourth Annual Convention of the Greenpoint-Williamsburg Coalition of Community Organizations, November 16, 1980 p. 42.

[39] Greenpoint Gazette, July 8, 1980 p.1.

[40] Greenpoint Gazette, December 23, 1980 p.1.

[41] This phrase was used by Jesse Jackson when he ran for the Presidency. It referred to his constituents. GWCOCO pre-dated Jackson's concept.

[42] This is a phrase used by David Dinkins, former Mayor of the City of New York in reference to New York City's culturally diverse population.

CHAPTER 6

THE COALITION'S DECLINE

In November 1981, the Coalition's fifth and final convention was held. It was evident by the planning of this event that the Coalition was disintegrating. Indicators of its decline include the scheduling of the fifth convention for the evening of a weekday with a shortened agenda. Conventions of previous years were held on Sunday afternoons, and often ran into the evening. Furthermore, the printed program for the fifth convention was not as elaborate as those from prior years. It had not been professionally printed, there were no photographs, and no paid advertisements. This chapter examines the factors which led to the organization's downfall, and discusses the state of member organizations at this time. Finally, the involvement of the Coalition's leaders and staff in its demise will also be presented.

REAGANOMICS

By 1980, Greenpoint-Williamsburg had experienced the first round of CETA job reductions. With the election of Ronald Reagan and the implementation of supply side economics, federal money, which was funding programs in local communities, disappeared. Both the Coalition and community organizations that existed because of CETA were vulnerable to these cuts in funding. Around the same time that the Coalition's grant from the Law Enforcement Assistance Agency (LEAA) was coming to an end with no hope for renewal, many of its member organizations were also in financial crisis as CETA was phased out. Although money was a continuous problem, all of these groups were now struggling for survival, and searching for alternative sources of funding. One organizer recalled,

> Funding was always a problem for the Coalition. It seems like we never had enough. I think we really worked hard with the little that we had. By the end we had to do fund raising for our salaries. The financial situation was very bleak. [Eventually], the funding stopped and we couldn't afford to pay the rent anymore, and we weren't getting any programs, and it just died.

The LEAA grant had given the Coalition a period of financial security. As a result of the lack of LEAA funds, the Coalition's staff found itself spending more time attempting to raise money, and less on community issues. Another organizer described,

> Toward the end we were trying to concentrate a lot on developing money cause we knew it was running out. That hurt us a lot because the people were used to us going out, doing leadership development, helping them define their issues. Then it came to the point where we couldn't give people that attention. We weren't as visible throughout the district as we were a few years earlier.

This hurt the Coalition because it was not as prominent and did not have the public presence it once enjoyed in the community.

DIVISIONS WITHIN THE COALITION

A divisive force occurred in the Coalition when one of its presidents was elected to the Area Policy Board to represent Greenpoint-Williamsburg. The Community Development Agency (CDA) replaced community corporations with the responsibility of selecting programs to fund with anti-poverty money. CDA divided New York City into smaller districts called area policy boards. Elections are held in each of these districts and the elected representatives allocate funds within their community.

One of the Coalition's presidents, who held this office from November 1979 to November 1980, was elected to the Area Policy Board. At this point in time, most community organizations in Greenpoint-Williamsburg had experienced a reduction of CETA workers and were awaiting CETA's complete elimination. In an attempt to prevent their dissolution, community organizations were exploring alternative sources of funding, without which, many of them would close. CDA was a potential pool of money for these groups. Many community organizations in Greenpoint-Wiliiamsburg applied to CDA to fund specific projects. The Coalition itself, did not apply to CDA since many of its member groups had submitted proposals and the Coalition did not want to compete with its member groups for money. The president of the Coalition and member of the Area Policy Board, however, found herself in the awkward position of selecting and awarding these grants to certain organizations over others. CDA did not have enough of money to fund all the organizations that applied. Instead of serving as a uniting force as she did with the Coalition, she embraced some groups and rejected others. This process created problems within the Coalition since some organizations were funded by CDA and others were not. Many of the Coalition's leaders and delegates were quite angry with this president to the extent that in November 1980, they elected another leader as president of the Coalition.

RE-ORGANIZATION

In 1980, the grant that the Coalition received from the Law Enforcement Assistance Agency (LEAA) was extended for one year with less money than the original appropriation. The organization was forced to reduce its personnel and administrative costs. The Coalition moved its office from Central Williamsburg to Greenpoint. Prior to these budget changes going into effect, there were 8 full-time organizers employed by the Coalition. One left for other employment, and one had to be terminated. The organizers' job titles and responsibilities were also changed in order to accomplish the personnel reduction. Instead of a youth organizer, a senior citizens organizer, and one community organizer working within each geographic (and ethnic) area of the Coalition (six organizers for six areas of the Coalition), organizing staff would now have specialties. Responsibilities were divided into the following distinct categories: civilian patrols, block and civic associations, non-residential and local fundraising, tenant associations and building seal-ups and demolitions, senior citizens, community youths.[1] Each of these six areas of responsibility were assigned to a full-time organizer. An organizer recalled,

There was a lot of conflict on the board around who was
going to be laid-off. Let's face it, that first staff was hired by
who knew who. Each area had input into hiring their own
organizer. So there were certain board members who were
very strong about not giving up their staff person. The
administrative staff had to fight with the board 'cause we
needed the skills. We needed to keep the good people. We
couldn't worry about doing anybody political favors or
keeping somebody's organizer.

STAFF LAY-OFFS

Discharging a community organizer from the Coalition did not occur
without some level of dissatisfaction from the Coalition's board and
member groups. The first organizer to be terminated because of fiscal
constraints worked in East Williamsburg. East Williamsburg was
comprised mostly of an African American community, and their
Coalition organizer was also black. The executive director evaluated the
past performance of the organizers, and made choices about who was
best qualified for the "new" positions. He believed that the staff person
responsible for East Williamsburg was the least effective. He
recommended to the Coalition's board of directors that this person be
laid-off. The board approved the director's recommendation.

At the next delegates' assembly, the organizer's mother, who was a
representative from Cooper Park Houses, announced that the "black"
organizer was laid-off and accused the Coalition of racism. A board
member was able to settle this matter by stating that the decision was not
based on race, and asking the assembly not to allow budget cuts to tear
apart the organization. It appeared by the end of the meeting that the
racial protest was isolated, and did not completely splinter the Coalition
along racial lines, but had some impact. A VISTA worker stated,

The first organizer laid-off was in East Williamsburg. I think
that did a lot to create bitterness among leaders and groups.
Troublemakers then made it a race issue.

As the budget got tighter, another staff person had to be terminated.
This lay-off went somewhat differently from the first case. At this point,
the Coalition could only support two full-time organizers. Three were
employed. The remaining three organizers from the original six
understood that the funding situation was bleak, and found employment

elsewhere. The presence of one additional organizer, however, created a situation in which, once again, the executive director had to decide which one to lay-off. He made his recommendation to the board of directors, however this time, the board rejected his suggestion and terminated another organizer. The board went against the director's suggestion because the staff person who the executive director wanted laid-off appealed to the board members who were responsible for hiring her and whom she worked with through the years. Other board members were then urged to vote to keep her. This is an additional case of the board exercising its control and disregarding the executive director's judgement.

PAYING DUES

In the context of personnel shrinkage and financial decline, the question of member organizations contributing payment to the Coalition arose again. As mentioned previously, this matter was discussed at an earlier stage of the Coalition's development, but was never implemented. Throughout the Coalition's existence, member groups were reluctant to make payment for the Coalition's services. At this point, as member groups lost CETA workers and experienced smaller operating budgets, they were not about to commit to contributing to a dues base for the Coalition. The Executive Director stated,

> The Board's overruling my recommendation to implement a
> dues structure was one of the key factors which led me to
> explore leaving to work for a national network where the role
> of the organizer was better understood.

He left the Coalition about ten months later to work at a project sponsored by the Industrial Areas Foundation (IAF).

Leaders and delegates were not accustomed to paying for community organizers and were not in the best financial shape to start. One of the Coalition's VISTA workers believed that "member organizations didn't want to pay dues because they thought we [the Coalition] were rich." The Coalition was made fiscally solvent by receiving funds from LEAA, but that was no longer the case by the last quarter of 1981. The Coalition's last president described the Coalition's final year,

> I recollect a lot of cut backs, city money and federal. A lot of

the organizations had the luxury of coming together with other organizations to work on issues. They suddenly had to worry about how to get money to survive. There were groups that actually went out of business. If you can't survive yourself in your own little corner of the community, how can you be part of larger issues? The Coalition lost funds too and member groups wouldn't and couldn't pay dues. It wasn't set up that way.

The Coalition declined as sources of public money disappeared. The community never learned to support the Coalition with private funds, and the Coalition never learned to be self-sufficient.

By the fifth convention, only 1 full-time organizer remained. When he too left the organization it marked the dissolution of the organizing staff. The leaders could not maintain the work of the Coalition without an organizing staff or the funds to continue, yet those leaders trained by the Coalition continued to be involved community residents.

Ultimately, the Coalition chose to go out of business for two major reasons. First, it did not want to compete with its member organizations for funding. Second, the Coalition would not re-define its objectives to fit the scope of programs outlined by benefactors. The Coalition faced destruction because of its dependency on powerful institutions for resources (Kraus 1984). In addition, based on their seminal work, Piven and Cloward (1977) would have predicted the Coalition's decline because of the way that it was formed. They argue that by emphasizing the creation of an organization, activist behavior is curtailed. Organizers miss "moments" or opportunities of insurgency when they are focused on building (and maintaining) an organization.

WHO SURVIVED and WHY

There were only a few community organizations which were formed in order to accept CETA job slots which survived after the dissolution of CETA and Reagan's cuts. They were able to obtain funding from other sources, such as the State and City of New York and private foundations. These organizations received money to carry out community-based programs for New York City's Departments of Housing Preservation and Development, Employment, and/or Youth Services. Moreover, some groups received smaller grants from State agencies and were part of New York State's supplemental budget. There purpose was to provide direct, social services in the form of community education, housing advocacy, youth recreation, and job training. The success of these organizations was due to their hiring a few college educated professionals under CETA who had the skills to write grant proposals, investigate sources of money, and handle government bureaucracy and officials. The outcome was a relationship between professionals and community workers that was successful in maintaining viable community organizations, at least for a time. As one community worker explained,

> In existence now are only about three good programs that started with CETA: People's Firehouse, National Congress of Neighborhood Women, and St. Nicholas Housing. Professional people came in and taught and that's how community people learn. Other groups didn't allow outsiders to be part of them.

This quotation notes that some of the professional staff came from outside of the community, while a few were community residents. The Coalition was not among this list of "good" organizations because of a decision made by its board members who represented those same groups that the Coalition would not compete with its members for funding. Furthermore, funding agencies were less likely to make appropriations for an organizing project than they were for direct, social services.

The economic recession of the 1990's has left the State and City of New York in fiscal crisis. These local governments can no longer support programs that the federal government has dropped. Community organizations face even worse funding conditions with few alternatives. The importance of the financial self-sufficiency of community organizations becomes apparent. Today, organizations must look to be supported by the private sector through grants, donations, and membership dues in which foundations and local institutions, such as churches and small businesses, as well as individuals can contribute. This method of funding also eliminates the paperwork and administrative demands on staff that government funding requires. In this way, the work of community organizations like the Coalition can continue regardless of the political climate and economic policy.

Notes

[1] This information was obtained from a memorandum to the staff which was not dated or signed entitled, "Brief Descriptions of the New Job Titles."

CHAPTER 7

COMMUNITY LIFE AFTER THE COALITION:
RETURNING TO A CONVENTIONAL SYSTEM OF COMMUNITY PARTICIPATION

With the cessation of the Greenpoint-Williamsburg Coalition of Community Organizations in 1982, the neighborhood was left with no ongoing source of grass roots, community power. In other words, there was no community wide organization attempting to improve living conditions and holding government accountable. In fact, the only entity available to address issues for both, Greenpoint and Williamsburg was the Community Board (Brooklyn's Community Board 1). Community boards are government groupings mandated by New York City's Charter. They are examples of legitimate power on a local level. They will be discussed in greater detail later.

This chapter will analyze the state of community power and citizen participation in Greenpoint-Williamsburg without the Coalition. This will include an examination of the contrasting approaches and functions of the community board and the Coalition, and why people, especially local leaders, chose to participate in them. The analysis will focus on these structures as models of community power. In addition, this chapter will discuss the position of civic organizations and block associations, organizations which constitute a more typical urban neighborhood atmosphere in the absence of the Coalition. Finally, the fact that some leaders of the Coalition decided to become members of the community board both before and after the Coalition closed will be examined for the purpose of identifying forums for exercising community power.

COMMUNITY LIFE WITHOUT A COALITION

With the termination of the Coalition, community activities in the Greenpoint-Williamsburg area were more typically reflective of New York City's system of government. When the Coalition ceased to exist, neighborhood problems and issues did not suddenly disappear with it. Like most urban neighborhoods in the 1980's and early 90's, Greenpoint-Williamsburg continued to encounter many problems. People expressed anger and frustration by crime, drugs, unaffordable housing, homelessness, hazardous waste and toxic dumping, to name a few. Residents persisted in raising these issues at the meetings of their many local civic organizations, however, their choices of action without a Coalition was limited to going before the community board, signing petitions, writing their elected representatives, and organizing spontaneous protests. Individuals could carry out all of these procedures, however their scale of operation was small compared to taking the issue to the Coalition and enlisting the support of the larger community along with its staff, leaders, and many organizations. Present day process works in such a way that residents make others aware of local problems, address the community board, and sometimes get the attention of local politicians. The testimony of locals given at the community board's public hearings is recorded and assigned to a committee for further work, or voted on for the board's support or opposition. This procedure does not empower people, but adds to their frustration. Moreover, displays of outrage by individuals or groups resulted in board suggestions that they be patient and work through the system. This description of local operations in Greenpoint-Williamsburg can also be applied to most neighborhoods and community boards in New York City.

Through the Coalition, the people of Greenpoint-Williamsburg could behave in radically different ways. They would "raise hell" by protesting, maintaining this tension over time, building relationships across ethnic and racial lines, and expecting that their concerns, which were presented as a specific demands, could and should be addressed by the power structure. The Coalition acted, while government, local elites, politicians, and the community board reacted, which usually set into motion several initiatives on the Coalition's agendas.

COMMUNITY BOARDS

With the adoption of the revision of New York City's Charter, the boroughs of the City were divided into smaller "community" districts, through which municipal services are delivered. Each district is managed by a community board which hires a District Manager. The community board is comprised of a maximum of fifty persons. One-half of the community board is appointed by the area's City Council representatives and the other half is determined by the Borough President. Community board appointees receive no monetary compensation for their service, but are reimbursed for expenses connected to their work.

On one level, the primary purpose of community boards is to give New York City's neighborhoods the opportunity to participate in local government. They are an outcome of decentralization. On a more subtle level, they function to pacify residents by absorbing protests, thus discouraging locals from moving directly to confront elected officials, commissioners, or City managers. Thus, unofficially, community boards serve as a screen for the Mayor and government officials. They act essentially as advisory councils to City agencies and the Mayor's office. They make recommendations to City government on the capital and expense budgets. In other words, they convey their construction and day-to-day spending priorities to the City's administration for a final decision. They also give guidance to the City on its Uniform Land Use Reform Process (ULURP). Community boards offer direction to government officials concerning zoning variances, changes, and proposed utilization of land by the City. They hold public hearings to introduce items to the community and assess the sentiment of residents before taking a public stand.

DISPARATE APPROACHES TO POWER

In carrying out its work, the Coalition occasionally was the impetus for the scheduling of public hearings by the community board. Leaders of the Coalition used the community board in a manner not envisioned by the City Charter. At times, the Coalition's leaders used these hearings to learn the board's position on a problem. The community board was rarely in a position to respond immediately to the Coalition's agenda of issues. The board would usually reply by scheduling additional hearings on the matter, or by agreeing to further examination of the problem at hand. For the most part, the Coalition knew that these were the probable yet limited reactions from the board, and if it was useful, the Coalition would use them to move their agenda and point out the inefficiency of the community board to get things done. The Coalition placed little value on the board's process, but frequently saw the community board hold public hearings on issues upon which the Coalition was already focused and acting. As part of a government bureaucracy, the community board was, in fact, unable to make quick decisions, be confrontive, or engage in civil disobedience. Usually, members of the board did not want to risk being embarrassed by going on record supporting or opposing an issue without being fully informed. The local politicians who appointed board members would frown on such mistakes. Moreover, many members of the community board used their position to obtain employment in City government, or to fulfill political aspirations. Therefore, members were cautious not to jeopardize possible employment opportunities.

The underlying political dynamics of the Coalition did not call for this kind of accountability. Coalition staff answered to their own leaders who were working on community concerns together. Ultimately, staff and leaders were responsible to the community groups that comprised the Coalition. The Coalition and Community Board are contrasting structures of community power representing elite and pluralist models. New York City's Charter states, "No person shall be appointed to or remain as a member of the board who does not have residence, business, professional or other significant interest in the district."[1] These "catch all" requirements allowed non-residents to sit on the board. People with special interests, such as aides to politicians, directors of social service agencies, and owners of local businesses could be found on the community board. The community board continues to be made-up of local elites. Politicians often co-opt people, their interests, and their activism by appointing them to the community board. On the other hand, the Coalition was a grass roots approach to power. It was comprised of ethnically mixed, and to some extent economically different groups of ordinary people who attempted to have some control over their lives and neighborhoods. Increased membership and participation by all groups was not only allowed, but continuously encouraged by most of the Coalition's leaders and organizers. The leadership believed that the more people involved, the more powerful they became, although not all leaders were comfortable with mass participation. These individuals would periodically leave the Coalition and join smaller civic or religious groups, or the community board.

THE CONTENTION OF DUPLICATION

Some members of the community board argued that there was no need for the Coalition, since the board represented the community. The assertion was that the Coalition reproduced the purpose of the community board. According to one member of the community board,

> [The Coalition] was unnecessary because of the organizational structure of the City of New York. The City Charter formalizes community participation through community boards. There was no role for the Coalition.

Another member added,

> I didn't see a particular role that [the Coalition] was playing. There was a search for certain issues...I think it was too heterogeneous to be meaningful. There was a skewing of purposes between what the community board was doing and what the Coalition was. The board, at least, had a clearly defined set of responsibilities. The Coalition was looking for things to do and to get involved in...It was searching for particular things to do.

The arguments presuppose a number of things. First, they presume that the community board, whose members were not elected by the community, actually represent the interests of the overall community. They may, in fact, be representing the agency, unit of government, or political official for whom they work, or political club or party which approved their placement on the board. Second, they speak as if the community board's membership is fluid, flexible, and open to large scale participation from residents. Third, they maintain that since the community board was designed for some degree of community input, its existence should somehow exclude the creation of additional and alternative systems of community participation by citizens. The quotations further suggest the difficulty these people have with the Coalition's form of participatory democracy which encourages scores of people to take part in shaping their community's future.

These respondents, and others like them believed that the Coalition accomplished little through the years. One person remarked,

> Some of the things they [the Coalition] claimed to do they
> didn't do. It was done by the community board.

Others claimed that the Coalition's approach to dealing with local problems was too radical. It was reported,

> [The Coalition's] radical thinking and activist mentality had
> no place here. You must get in the system and make changes.
> The role of protest is useful, but not everyday. The Coalition
> was never of any real significance.

This quotation points out a major difference between the community board and the Coalition. That is, the fact that the community board is part of New York City's system of government and therefore works within it, while the Coalition was outside of local government and therefore developed more extreme ways of attacking that system and embarrassing it into meeting the "people's" demands.

A former president of the Coalition had a dissimilar view concerning the roles of the community board and the Coalition. He said,

> The community board was more of a hazard than a help.
> They were part of the machine appointed by the Borough
> President. All the issues were supposed to go through them.
> The community board fought us like crazy. They wouldn't
> give us letters of support when we asked for them...They
> don't believe what I do. They think it's not nice to go against
> the policy of the City.

These statements clearly illustrate the divergent ideologies on community power that emerged in Greenpoint-Williamsburg. Interestingly, as the Coalition waned, some of its former leaders were found appointed to the community board. Weber's analysis of authority (1947) is useful here. The Coalition can be viewed as charismatic authority. After the decline of the Coalition, charisma diminished. Some charismatic leaders (who were attached to the Coalition), were routinized into positions of rational-legal authority (those appointed by politicians to the community board). This transition included individuals who perceived the community board as ineffective and problematic regarding the Coalition's goals. The next section will discuss this conversion.

THE EMERGENCE OF LEADERS THROUGH ACTION

Individuals who were leaders of the Coalition received training and learned skills which helped to build their individual and collective confidence. By observing others and through direct experience, many leaders came to be empowered by their participation in the Coalition. They asserted themselves with bureaucrats by interrupting City officials' presentations when it did not address the community's issues. They came to celebrate winning and engaged in more strategy when they were defeated. The process of going from being a working class or poor person who, for the most part, deferred to authority, to an activist who questioned authority and distrusted government and corporations involved many factors. Experiencing the effects of cuts in services through the years was one influence. Another was witnessing the negative response of people in authority to what community residents perceived as logical, humane requests. The Coalition helped crystallize into displeasure the ambivalence that many community people felt toward government bureaucracy. The Coalition provided a vehicle by which community people expressed themselves. The political consciousness of Coalition leaders was transformed. The Coalition not only provided the arena, but additional assistance as well. The Coalition's organizing staff involved leaders in researching issues, and held pre-meetings to prepare leaders for an upcoming action or assembly. As one leader expressed,

> You had your organizer there with you to go through the agenda which gave you more confidence [to run a meeting and to speak at meetings].

The few community residents who viewed the Coalition as duplicating the purpose of the community board also thought that the relationship between leaders and organizers was problematic. This perspective is summarized in the following remarks,

> [The organizers] were doing all the work while they were using figureheads really to do the thing...We had a president, but the president was a figurehead. [The executive director] was really the leader. We would have been better off having [the organizers] up-front and working with the community as

a whole, helping to achieve their goals rather than to put up
figureheads and give them notes telling them what we
accomplished. It wasn't very honest. The elected positions
were really pawns of the paid staff.

This is a classic analysis of the relationship between leaders and
organizers. It fails to address the fact that traditional community leaders
without a staff or organization, do not usually have the time or expertise
to gather information or develop position papers. This negative reaction
to organizers relates to a paternalistic view of grass roots leaders as
"simple folks" who are easily manipulated by those attempting to stir up
trouble. The people who make these assessments strongly oppose the
behavior of ordinary people attempting to challenge, disrupt, and bypass
the existing political system. These remarks were made by two
community board members. One is a career City bureaucrat who lives in
the community, and the other is also a resident and aide to a local
politician. Their view is that they know what is "good and best" for the
community and have regular access to the power structure. They,
ironically, were critical of the organizer's role but have no problem with
the practice that government staff support community board members.
The fact is that the leaders of the Coalition continued their community
activism after the organizers were gone. Leaders took their experiences,
skills, and social networks from the Coalition to their next arena of
community involvement. The importance of social networks here needs
to be highlighted. As a leader of the Coalition, even for a short period of
time, one became at least acquainted if not friendly with other
community leaders and organizations throughout Greenpoint and
Williamsburg. These relationships and contacts became important tools
for community work.

THE CONVERSION OF COMMUNITY LEADERS

As mentioned earlier, many of the Coalition's leaders were appointed
to the community board. Some sat on the community board, while also
serving as a member of the Coalition's board of directors. Others used the
Coalition as a stepping stone to community board membership. Still other
Coalition leaders moved to the community board after the Coalition
ceased to exist. There were several reasons for these transitions. One was
that some former Coalition leaders were more comfortable with the
board's routinized style of leadership participation than with the

Coalition's more radical, unpredictable approach. Appointments of Coalition leaders to the community board occurred because the Coalition gave individuals a way to be noticed by politicians for selection. In some cases politicians co-opted the activism of leaders by appointing them to the community board or as their aide.

Another major reason for joining the community board was that after the Coalition stopped operating, the community board remained the only entity to address community-wide issues. Thus, leaders without a coalition moved to the only other "big show in town." A former president of the Coalition reported,

> I think that they specifically went from the Coalition to the community board because people liked and enjoyed being involved in the community. I think it was a place to be because it was a place for people involved in issues in the community. I think [it was a place] for some of us who didn't have a place to go [after the Coalition]. There are a number of people that did go from the Coalition to the community board. I think they felt it was a place to also bring your expertise. What we gained from being part of the Coalition we were able to use by being part of the community board. My latest stop in community work is the community board. I feel it's a culmination of [my career]. I'm on that board with people who I came part of that distance with. I think we're able to broaden our horizons and lend the expertise we have to that board. And part of it comes from how involved we were with the Coalition.

Finally, other activists gave up their community activism for employment or funding through the power structure, and found the community board to be the place where they could protect their personal interests. Former leaders of the Coalition who were not appointed to the community board continued to be involved in the block or civic association which they represented at the Coalition. The relationships they developed through the Coalition continue to be beneficial to their community work.

COMMUNITY INVOLVEMENT AS A BOARD MEMBER

Former leaders of the Coalition who, at the time of this writing were members of the community board, recognize the different approaches to

dealing with City government represented by the Coalition and the
community board. For most, appointment to the community board ended
the more radical approach and participatory strategies developed to
confront those in power. Former Coalition leaders found themselves
working within the system. A past president of the Coalition who later sat
on the community board also remarked,

> You're on a different level when you're on the board. It's a
> different kind of power. The Coalition had people power.
> This, together with the power of the people on the
> community board, could have been remarkable because the
> Coalition did bring in numbers when it came to
> organizational power. The Coalition wasn't into pussy
> footing around with the Borough President and the Mayor.
> They were into the real guts, the people. You need somebody
> at the next level to be the guy that [works the bureaucracy]
> and I think that's people on the community board. I think the
> whole thing could have come together.

There is the realization on the part of this person that the Coalition and
the community board could have worked together. However, this
individual developed this view not as a president of the Coalition, but
years later as a member of the community board.

The problem now for some leaders in Greenpoint-Williamsburg is
that there is no effective vehicle for organizing people. The statement of a
Coalition leader illustrates this point.

> The only benefit I see being on the community board is you
> sometimes get first hand information...I'm on the community
> board now and they hate my guts. They never liked the way I
> do things. I take direct action, and they go through the
> bullshit paper work. Red tape that you never get nowhere. It
> doesn't work. I tell them what to do, "you want to
> demonstrate?" I'm like a thorn in their asses. I'm always
> there...They try to remove me. They check my
> attendance...Believe it or not now I'm on no committees [of
> the community board]. They won't appoint me. A lot of nice
> people, but their humps.

As a member of the community board people are forced to follow
bureaucratic procedure. However, this person, like others quoted later,
was politically transformed by his experience with the Coalition, has

remained an activist, and continues to believe that tactics such as picketing the homes of politicians or stopping traffic during rush hour are the best approaches to resolving community problems.

As mentioned previously, the board's decision making ability is limited. The community board submits recommendations on items to the Mayor's office or various government agencies. One board member said,

> The community board I see now, we can only propose something. We really are pawns. We are a smoke screen. [Decisions] are really up to the Borough President [and others]...If we were so powerful, we wouldn't be fighting [about issues] for ten years.

Community activists, through groups like the Coalition, express opposition to proposals by City government. They can change the final outcome. Another board member commented,

> The potential power of the Coalition is much greater [than that of the community board]. The board is limited. It's only an advisory group and can only do certain things. It's a decision maker in an advisory sense. Most issues community boards deal with are minimal...unimportant and non-controversial issues. But in the big areas, the important issues, community boards are often bypassed, overlooked, and ignored. The Greenpoint Shelter is an example.

This person's reference to the Greenpoint Shelter is an illustration of a recommendation made by the community board that was ignored by government. During the 1980's, New York City was opening barrack type shelters for the homeless. One site selected was a vacant building which had been Greenpoint Hospital. The community opposed a homeless shelter, and the community board voted against a homeless shelter. The Mayor was committed to opening shelters for the homeless, and he did so regardless of the recommendations of community boards or community reaction.

ETHNIC AND RACIAL CONFLICT

As discussed throughout this book, the communities of Greenpoint and Williamsburg are culturally diverse. The structure of the Coalition was deliberately created to include tin the organization the various ethnic groups which comprise the area. The Coalition not only brought together the "mosaic"[2] of people from Greenpoint and Williamsburg, but also promoted and fostered positive relationships. Social networks, which were multi-ethnic, multi-racial, and multi-age, developed. These local networks were often the first occasion for people of different colors and cultures, who shared the same community, to build relationships. Without a Coalition, there is no organization or local institution which intentionally builds relationships across ethnic, racial, age, and to some extent class lines. These groups are represented on the community board. There are agents from the Hasidic, Italian, Hispanic, African American, Irish and Polish communities. However, there is polarization on the board. These groups do not work together in harmony. In fact, individuals who participated in the Coalition and the community board cite racial conflict as a major problem on the community board, and the ability to integrate people as a major success of the Coalition. One such person expressed,

> I wish the Coalition had lasted a lot longer because, quite frankly, one of the struggles we're having on the community board, one of the ongoing struggles is a racial one. It seems to be that consistently the Italian community will vote with the Hasidics for no particular reason. We're trying to ask [them to vote with the Hispanics on issues that aren't important to the Italians]. We've gotten into some conspiratorial thinking regarding Youth Services money. I've been very unhappy over the last couple of years with some of my Italian friends.

Another person in a similar position said,

> I do believe in a Coalition. I think that's the only way that things work. A Coalition to let all people be involved in it and all aspects of problems in the community. There was a sense of happiness too because we did things together. At that time I didn't hear anything racial...Half the community board meetings are so racial. You never get anything done. It's so mistrusting. [People are always looking for ethnic representation on committees]. When you're dealing with money [there's conflict].

Tasks before the community board often fail to be unifying. In fact, they tend to be fractionalizing. This is particularly the case when the board develops budgets, or recommends that public money be awarded to certain community organizations over others. This process sets a tone of competition among ethnic groups which leads to divisions and conflict. It could be argued that the central administration of City government is shielded by this process. Community board members are segregated and spar with each other which deflects attention away from City Hall and government agencies. On the other hand, GWCOCO understood, for the most part, that funding decisions divide the community. The Coalition's perspective focused on quality of life issues in "our" neighborhood. It stressed unity of purpose. The Coalition tried not to become involved with matters which selected some of its member groups over others. In fact, the Coalition itself would not compete with its member groups for funding and perished as a result of this practice.

There is recognition that community groups like the Coalition are necessary for the viability of urban neighborhoods. This view is conveyed in the following quotation,

> A lot of things that the Coalition worked on are still in effect, and a lot of the groups that took part in it internalized it. But there's no one out there now to bring together the ethnic, racial, and economic issues. There's no solid group out there fighting for any kind of funding, or fighting any of the [City] budget issues...Basically, there's no one out there pushing.

This analysis of the Coalition illustrates that community organizations can prevent the further splintering of race and class relations which result from increased economic challenges.

As urban America confronts the struggle between diminishing resources and increasing needs, grass roots organizations can affect the outcome of policy decisions and the allocation of capital.

Notes

[1] "City Government in the Community," Chapter 70, Section 2800 of the New York City Charter as amended December 31, 1989, p.288.
[2] This is a term used by David Dinkins, former Mayor of the City of New York, to refer to the many diverse ethnic groups that comprise the City.

CHAPTER 8

WOMEN AND COMMUNITY

The participation of women in the creation, leadership, and activities of the Coalition occurred at a much larger scale than women's involvement in local political clubs or the Community Board. For the most part, women were a numerical majority as participants in Coalition events and actions, and also in elected leadership positions. Women involved in the Coalition worked on a variety of local issues including the renovation of local parks, adequate sewers, more police protection, the maintenance of investment practices, schools, and essential city services.

This chapter examines women's participation in the Coalition. It begins by summarizing research which focuses on the role of women in community and critically evaluating community studies regarding an analysis of women. This chapter then discusses the community work of women in Greenpoint-Williamsburg by presenting a profile of women's informal and formal activism including their involvement in the Coalition.

WOMEN'S PLACE IN COMMUNITY STUDIES

Women play a major part in the everyday life of working class, ethnic neighborhoods. Yet, researchers have given little attention to the activities of women in neighborhoods. Past research on urban neighborhoods has been based on a male perspective, and has not examined the role of women (Gans 1962; Kornblum 1974; Liebow 1967; Rieder 1985; Suttles 1968; Whyte 1955). Whyte, for example, examines "corner boys" and college boys." Gans notes that most of his data was gathered from and about men, and that his presentation of peer group society emphasizes men. Liebow focuses on "streetcorner men" and Kornblum presents the largely male worlds of union and local political party organizations. When women are discussed in these studies they are presented only in relationship to men.

In most studies on urban neighborhoods, women have been viewed in terms of their traditional role, working inside the home as wives and mothers. Their participation in community beyond this has gone largely unrecognized. Lofland (1975) argues that in literature on urban sociology, women are merely "there," that is part of the scene but not part of the action. The plots of studies move around them, rather than focusing on them. According to Lofland, the "thereness of women" is a result of approaches to the study of community and the gender of the researcher. For Lofland, the emphasis on community as a model of social organization creates a problem of conceptualization for the researcher. The researcher's view of urban forms is confined to those areas in which the model can be applied. Other possible urban forms are, therefore, not investigated. Thus, the use of this model of community points researchers to empirical settings where women are only "there" and directs them away from settings where women are present. Many researchers have overlooked women's activities in studies of urban settings. This is particularly the case for low income women because researchers have investigated formal positions and physical locations in communities in which women have not been participants.

Since most researchers are men, they have difficulty gaining access to women's groups and obtaining interviews with women. This dilemma is intensified in low income communities in which communication between the sexes is more traditional and, therefore, somewhat limited. As Gans (1962) notes, a woman spending time with a man who is not a relative may be viewed as engaging in inappropriate behavior. It is, therefore, not surprising that sociological research on urban life presents "corner boys," "college boys," and "streetcorner men." It is only recently that we see social scientists, who are women, studying ethnic, low income women in communities (DeSena 1990; Gittell and Shtob 1980; Haywoode 1989; 1991; Kaplan 1982; Kibria 1990; Naples 1998; McCourt 1977; Schoenberg and Dabrowski 1978; Schoenberg 1981; Susser 1982; 1988). These studies demonstrate that women's community work is central to the viability of neighborhoods and to the quality of life. The following review of literature illustrates this new genre.

McCourt (1977) analyzes the political activism of working class women in Chicago. She compares women involved in "assertive community organizations" (social action oriented) to non-active women. McCourt contends that the active women are moving from a traditional working class lifestyle to a more modern one in which they participate in the world beyond their families and homes. Membership in assertive community organizations is, for these women, their first involvement in politics. Many women stated that they joined an organization to fight a neighborhood problem but they were also encouraged to join and to participate by a member of the group. Active women experienced a sense of empowerment and believed that they could work toward resolving local problems.

Like McCourt, Gittell and Schtob (1980) investigate the political participation of working class women through their involvement in community organizations that are social action oriented and confront political agencies. Findings by McCourt and Gittell and Schtob challenge previous studies which argue that men are more political than women, and that working class women in particular, are uninvolved in politics (Rainwater 1959; Komarovsky 1964).

Kaplan's study of Barcelona, Spain (1982) is an historical example of working class women's collective action. Kaplan examines women's mobilization around social issues in the early 1900's which include: child molestation, wages, and war shortages. She explains that women organized their intended actions by neighborhood. "In their neighborhoods they experienced the power of networks created through years of shared tasks" (Kaplan 1982, 553).

Schoenberg and Dabrowski (1978) examine factors which promoted or inhibited working class women's involvement in community. They found that paid work is a requirement for the community participation of working class women. They also note that part-time paid work and part-time volunteer work is the combination most favored by working class women. Schoenberg and Dabrowski conclude that "paid work, particularly when it is part-time, may serve the same function for the working class women that education did for the middle class women in social role expansion" (1978, 19).

Naples (1998) studies low income women who were community workers in anti-poverty programs from 1964 to 1984. She finds that these women workers were committed to community work long before it was recognized as such. Most of these women performed unpaid work. According to Naples, the women experienced their work as an attempt to maintain and build community. There were various motivations cited by women for engaging in community work which include: resistance to racism, concern for children's health and welfare, and concern for deteriorating conditions in neighborhoods. Like McCourt and Gittell and Schtob, Naples finds that the experience of community work contributed to these women's sense of personal and political power.

Susser (1982; 1988) contributes to this discussion on the political activism of working class women through her study of Norman Street, which is actually the community of Greenpoint-Williamsburg in Brooklyn. Susser documents women's involvement in collective actions. They formed and participated in block associations, and tenants associations, and organized residents around local issues, such as: health care, day care, the quality of education, the prevention of the demolition of housing, and closing of a firehouse. According to Susser, women's collective action was possible because of the informal, social groups and linkages they formed while carrying out daily responsibilities. Susser concludes that the collective organizing of working class women has increased recently in an attempt to maintain few remaining services, as employment opportunities continue to decline for the working class. Like Susser, my study of Greenpoint (DeSena 1990) includes women's activities as part of an informal network in defending the neighborhood from residential integration. This research will be discussed later.

Kibria (1990) discusses the activities of Vietnamese immigrant women in the life of their ethnic community in the United States. She finds that these women play a powerful role in the ethnic community where they are organized around two central activities: the exchange of resources among households, and the mediation of domestic conflicts. Women exchange food, material goods, services, and information about "good buys" and employment opportunities. These immigrant women have also developed strategies for coping with male authority and violence in the family. At times the group would support or encourage a woman's decision to leave her husband. At other times, the women's group would bring pressure to bear on the husband by disseminating information about his behavior throughout the community by way of this network of women. Women were able to affect the reputations of people in the community and in some cases had an impact on their behavior. These women "bargain with patriarchy," but do not undermine traditional boundaries of family relations within the Vietnamese community.

Haywoode's work (1989) deals with working class feminism. She contends that during the 1970's and early 1980's, a new form of political organization developed which was based on existing, informal neighborhood networks. According to Haywoode, women have always been members of local networks, and like Susser, Haywoode argues that this places them in a position to organize around neighborhood issues. Working class women can become more political in the process. For Haywoode, working class women live in worlds beyond the nuclear family which includes: the extended family, the church, the neighborhood, and local organizations. Haywoode agrees that to a large extent, researchers have missed the activities of working class women. For Haywoode, new political organizations are being developed based on these existing, informal networks which women have formed in their neighborhoods.

Women's community activism, both progressive and conservative are central to the viability and quality of life of neighborhoods. As indicated, the social science literature presently documents low income women as community organizers and participants of all kinds of neighborhood struggles. Women in Greenpoint-Williamsburg are no exception in that they strategize to maintain community. The ways in which this is done will be discussed.

WOMEN'S INFORMAL ACTIVISM

In Greenpoint-Williamsburg residents use a series of informal strategies aimed at preserving the local culture (DeSena 1990; 1994). Women are the "defenders" of the neighborhood. They act as local surveillants or block watchers by taking responsibility for ongoing observation of street life in the neighborhood. Since crime has become such a topic of interest in urban neighborhoods, residents of some neighborhoods discuss crime prevention and hold public forums. Others hire professional security services. Still others create local patrols and form citizen policing groups. In Greenpoint-Williamsburg, crime prevention is viewed as a shared responsibility among local women who actively engage in surveillance and expect reciprocal behavior of each other.

As in most urban neighborhoods, people are concerned about homes being burglarized. One preventive strategy used by residents of Greenpoint-Williamsburg is to alert neighbors of their absence. Residents attempt to prevent the occurrence of burglaries rather than reacting after an incident has happened. Thus, surveillance operates in a variety of ways, but primarily as an informal process. One is by residents informing their neighbors when they are going out for the day or on vacation, and by asking them to watch their property while they are gone.

It is women asking their women neighbors to watch their property while they are out for the day or on vacation.

Another way that women carry out surveillance is by keeping an eye on children (both their own and others), the behavior of young adults and adolescents, the homes of neighbors, and the actions of those passing by. They confront suspicious events either directly or by calling the police, and often solicit help from other residents by ringing their door bells and stopping people on the street. Women in Greenpoint and Central Williamsburg have also created and maintain a local network in which they serve as informal brokers in the local housing market, where they are involved in renting available apartments, selling houses, and recruiting potential tenants and buyers. This information is conveyed orally through a network of women who interact in the street, at social and religious functions, and at civic meetings. As part of their daily routine, women will meet as they shop, walk children to and from school, go to and from work, and attend meetings in the community at night. It is during these informal occasions that matters concerning the neighborhood or specific people or issues are discussed, strategized, and planned.

Resident homeowners go about finding a tenant by an informal network through which they notify family, friends, and neighbors that an apartment is available. Consequently, if a member of the network knows someone who is "in the market" for an apartment, s/he will recommend this individual to the owner. These informants are overwhelmingly women. Individuals seeking apartments are thus "sponsored" by locals to homeowners. Those who act as informants are similar to the homeowner in terms of ethnic background and social class.

To a large extent, local women control who obtains housing. They "pass along the word," regarding the availability of housing to family, friends, and neighbors. In this way, these women have replaced local realtors. This is an important source of informal power for local women, especially since homeownership is probably the largest financial asset of many families. Residents are not willing to trust anyone with what represents their life's work and savings. Women also play the role of sponsor for neighborhood residents interested in new housing, and also for those seeking to move into the community from other areas.

Although the discussion to this point has focused on local surveillance and a housing network, the local women's network involves other aspects of neighborhood life as well. When women meet each other daily as they shop, attend church, or walk children to and from school. information about the neighborhood or specific people, issues or events is passed (Stack 1974; Haywoode 1989; Kibria 1990). They exchange local news. Women discuss who is moving and what that means for the neighborhood or for friends and family who would like to buy a house or rent an apartment on that block. They also discuss such topics as where the best sales are, what they new priest is like, who has recently been robbed. Women's networks in communities have been trivialized as "chatter" and mistakenly viewed as having no purpose. Haywoode states that "women build community through the activities of everyday life...What may appear to the casual observer as idle chatter, or time-wasting gossip, is really the creation of a network of social exchange, information sharing, informal contacts, and the building of social cohesion" (1989, 84-85).

WOMEN'S FORMAL ACTIVISM

In addition to examining informal networks, this chapter will also discuss the role of women in neighborhood institutions. Women in Greenpoint-Williamsburg are also members of formal organizations like the Coalition. In fact, the majority of those who attend meetings of church groups, block associations, civic organizations, and rallies related to neighborhood issues are women. Women are usually the ones who organize these meetings and mobilize resources. They recruit people to attend meetings and rallies by creating and distributing newsletters and flyers, and "talking-up" issues. Women also lobby elected officials, and members of the Community and School Boards about local problems and development plans. In other words, women are the rank and file of neighborhood activism. Women are also found in some leadership positions, serving as presidents, members of the boards of directors, and executive constituents of community organizations.

One area of neighborhood life that is rarely discussed in community studies is the role of religion. Suttles (1968), for example, notes that most Italians in the Addams area are Roman Catholic. One Catholic Church he describes in particular, which Italians call "their church," is considered the most powerful institution in the area. It is the scene of conflict resolution between Italians and other groups. Suttles does not deal with church involvement in neighborhood defense, nor does he discuss the recreational activities offered by the Church to local youth. The studies by Gans (1962), Susser (1982), and Kornblum (1974) hardly mention the existence of religious facilities. In contrast, Howell (1973) notes that part of his participant observation occurred at Sunday services, especially those of the Southern Baptist and Pentecostal denominations. We can infer from Howell's discussion that he had some familiarity with these churches. Whyte's study of Cornerville (1955) includes an extensive description of the "festa" and an analysis of this even as part of working class culture. This activity links religion with local community in southern Italy. The "festa" celebrates the feast of the patron saint of a particular town in Italy.

Women's involvement in religious institutions on a local level is certainly an under-represented area of inquiry in the social sciences. The Catholic Church is a major part of the lives of Greenpoint-Williamsburg's residents, especially since many children attend Catholic elementary schools administered by local parishes. While the Catholic Church does not permit women to become priests or to hold positions of power within the hierarchy, ironically, a close examination of Church activities reveals that on a local level, women parishioners are responsible for the viability of religious and Church events. Those who attend masses and other religious functions are overwhelmingly women. Women serve as members of parish committees, work at bingo sessions and other fund raisers, cook for parish receptions, clean and change altar linens, serve as Eucharistic ministers and lectors, and organize and staff programs for the poor. In Greenpoint-Williamsburg, Catholic Churches would literally collapse if not for the voluntary work of local women.

Local electoral politics is another area of neighborhood life where most researchers have not recognized the role of women. However, there is evidence that they play an active role. Kornblum (1974) notes that Mexican women were very involved in the local electoral process in south Chicago. They canvassed areas prior to election day, and in some cases served as precinct organizers. Moreover, Haywoode (1989) points out that the political role of women emerges in situations which can not be handled in traditional ways.

In Greenpoint-Williamsburg, women go from door to door to have petitions signed so local candidates can be placed on the ballot. It is also women who work at polling places on election days and distribute campaign literature for various candidates. Furthermore, as political patronage and the role of political parties as employers continue to decrease, it is probable that women will emerge increasingly in leadership positions in local politics. This is because women view local elections as a community event and will work for no monetary compensation.

The Coalition provided an arena whereby women's unrecognized activism was supported and made visible. Women were given a place in the Coalition to present their skills through activism and public forums. Through the Coalition, women's community work was moved from being "there" (Lofland 1975), in the background of community life, to more formal, public arenas. Women chaired community meetings, agitated elected officials and government representatives, and served as President and other executive officers of the Coalition. Women learned to assert themselves and to engage in public speaking, a practice which is uncomfortable for most women according to Deborah Tannen (1990). With every assertion, these women were empowered.

This investigation of women in Greenpoint-Williamsburg suggests that women create community (Haywoode 1991; DeSena 1990). They do it through their everyday activities. The activism described in Chapters 3 and 5 reflect the citizenship of neighborhood women. The influence of June Price on the neighborhoods's achievements can not be stressed enough. Women organized Conselyea Street Block Association, and fought for a day care center. Women were also involved in the struggle to preserve housing when S&S Corrugated planned expansion, and fought to maintain fire protection. In some of these cases, local women were the organizers, working behind the scenes.

Greenpoint-Williamsburg's CETA program hired mostly neighborhood women. The program offered women employment opportunities, and gave married women the option to be re-integrated into the labor force. These jobs were located in the neighborhood, close to women's homes, and allowed women the flexibility to fetch a child after school, to be home before their husbands, and to carry out tasks to maintain the household. As CETA employees, many women found themselves being paid for community work that they had done in the past as a volunteer. CETA paid women to continue to build community. A former CETA employee remarked,

> I think most of the women in CETA held positions that were
> not of power. It goes in line with the CETA titles. A lot of
> people that filled the key positions were men. A lot of them
> that played support roles were women. Since you have
> more peons, most of them were women. A lot of the women,
> they never worked before. It was an opportunity for women
> to get paid for doing the work that they were doing as
> volunteers.

For many local women, CETA prepared them for regular

employment. CETA jobs were completely terminated in 1980, and many women participants moved on to other jobs and to higher education. However, many of these women activists remained involved in community issues. Local women are an observed majority in community organizing efforts regardless of the ethnicity or social class of others involved. In other words, women cross racial, ethnic, and economic lines when organizing around community issues. One woman commented,

> Women played a key role in leadership, but were never recognized. The ones who were usually concerned about activities in the community were women who had kids, and they always wanted life to be better for the kids. So they participated in PTA's, in civic groups, they did the fund raising, they do the issue organizing. Most of them were smart enough to do the writing, so they would do the letters and they were considered "secretaries." But we know secretaries carry a lot of power. I think the concerns of women are around children. It could be anything from a street light to being afraid of a kid getting hurt on the corner, to better police protection. I don't think their fathers go out there and fight like the women do.

In Greenpoint-Williamsburg, women are in the forefront of community involvement and activism.

One community organization which emerged as a result of the CETA contract, and was a member organization of the Coalition, was National Congress of Neighborhood Women (NCNW). This organization offered leadership training and a community based college program (Haywoode 1991). Many women who were CETA workers were also enrolled in the college program. This program developed the skills of its participants with an emphasis on community work. According to one local woman,

> The basics of NCNW's programs were put together by women who worked in CETA jobs. CETA allowed them to explore educational opportunities or sharpen their skills for new jobs and organizing. Everybody wanted to be a community organizer because they wanted to make their neighborhood better. A lot of people at the Congress came together to accomplish a life long goal because a lot of women quit school for a number of reasons. They were told they weren't smart enough. They got pregnant, or they got

married and were in traditional roles. You stay home, you
raise the kids. You don't work and you don't go to school.
[With this program], they had the opportunity to change and
to do something better.

Among the many activities involved in building community was
women's participation in the Coalition. Many of the women who
graduated from NCNW's program are found as leaders and activists of
the Coalition. These women used the skills developed in the college
program for Coalition activities. They were elected to the Coalitions's
board of directors, including the position of President. Neighborhood
women chaired committees on a variety of local issues, and debated with
representatives of City government at public forums.

Women were empowered and also transformed by their participation
in the Coalition. Noschese (1991) remarks in Metropolitan Avenue, her
film about women's activism in Greenpoint-Williamsburg.

> ...These women who took leadership in their community to
> fight for things they believed in, and in the process...they
> developed an inner strength inside themselves. And they,
> regardless of whether they won or they lost, or what the issue
> was, it sort of changed their lives. Just the fact that they
> acted to fight for what they believed in. That is sort of what I
> guess power is about...But what they ...decided was that
> something meant something to them...and they decided to
> work for it and work for other people and it really changed
> them. It changed them like nothing in their lives had
> changed them before.

Many maintain the cross racial relationships and networks formed by
their involvement in the Coalition. Moreover, many continued their
community work after the Coalition's decline and took with them a
different view of politics, government, race relations, and the workings of
a democratic system, that developed from their activism. As one woman
expressed,

> A lot of things that the Coalition worked on are still in effect.
> But there's no one out there not to bring together ethnic, racial,
> and economic groups. There's no solid group out there
> fighting for any kind of funding, or fighting any of the budget
> issues.

They also acquired skills from Coalition activities, such as public speaking and analyses of power, which served them as they carried on community work. Former Coalition participants who are women are presently found in various local settings. Some remained active in the community organizations that they represented in the Coalition. Others have devoted themselves to resolving environmental hazards in Greenpoint-Williamsburg. Some, who worked on planning the physical and social environments under the auspices of the Coalition, proceed in their efforts. Women leaders of the Coalition have entered local electoral politics by being elected to public office, or to the School Board, hired as a political aide, or appointed to the Community Board. They continue to be informed and shaped politically by their activist experiences.

This chapter on women and community raises a major theoretical question concerning women's position as it relates to their connection to community life and organizations. One explanation is that patriarchy places women in this role. Under patriarchy, women are the protectors of hearth and home and the living conditions of one's neighborhood is included as part of women's work: Even as women's traditional roles expand to include full-time, paid employment, community life remains a component of women's responsibility, along with domestic chores and childcare. This view presents women as passive receiver of patriarchal rule.

An additional interpretation of women's connection to community is that the value of women's work continues to be grossly underestimated. Like family, community is central to the quality of life of human beings. Community life has a major impact on the development and condition of human life. From the standpoint of society, economics, the accumulation of capital, and electoral politics are the arenas of power, prestige, and importance. Yet this view is based on a male paradigm, probably because men typically hold these positions. It is, however, "women's work" in the community and family that reach and affect most people on an everyday basis. The power, prestige, and importance associated with controlling one's physical and social environments has gone unrecognized by scholars and society.

Finally, this chapter indicates the political involvement of women and reconceptualizes political behavior to include community activism. The women studied in Greenpoint-Williamsburg may or may not partake in the electoral process on a regular basis, but are clearly involved in shaping and controlling their local environments for themselves and their families. Their actions, informal and formal, demonstrate that they are engaged in ongoing and dynamic political activity.

CHAPTER 9

CONCLUSIONS

The previous chapters described a number of community problems that the Coalition attempted to resolve. Although it could be argued that this study is particularistic, implications of theoretical significance can be extrapolated. This case study bridges everyday experience with a macroanalysis of the social structure. It gives social scientists a glimpse into the potential that community organizations have in creating critical consciousness, and altering people's awareness of politics, race relations, class position, feminism, and citizen participation. This study also presents a model of neighborhood organization which utilizes existing, traditional community institutions for its membership base.

In Greenpoint-Williamsburg, the process of struggle politicized those involved. In the initial stage of settling any grass roots issue, residents turned to legitimate authorities including local, elected politicians, offices of City government and City services, to remedy the situation. In many instances, these officials took no action. Residents were surprised that their government was unresponsive to their needs (Gibbs 1982 and Krauss 1989 and 1993 describe similar accounts). They experienced a contradiction between their belief in government and government's lack of support. After this period of disillusionment, the process of politicization began. Informed by the non-reaction of government, residents realized that they had to develop tactics which would require the system to address the community's needs. The Coalition was the mechanism used by residents and their community organizations to strategize and implement protest activities in order to achieve their goals. Political consciousness was altered in that prior to the existence of the Coalition, people believed the proverb "you can't fight City Hall." However, this notion was recast by the Coalition to "what will we fight City Hall about." The process of struggle converted residents from a state of passive acceptance of policy decisions to one where they demanded more attention and accountability from government and politicians. Those involved in this transition were housewives, welfare mothers, retired union members, young adults, former gang members, and local merchants. When the authorities ignored or resisted the community's demands, residents persisted, re-strategized and served as the watchdogs of government. This process of politicization was also extended to electoral politics. People gained an increased sensibility of electoral politics. They were interested in information about candidates in local races and in school board elections, and some residents openly supported particular candidates and worked on his or her campaign. This transition of political consciousness suggests the capability of community organizations to work as agents of social change from below.

The experience of coalition building also enhanced race relations in the community of Greenpoint-Williamsburg. In an earlier analysis of Greenpoint (DeSena 1990), it was established that residents used a series of informal strategies to "protect one's turf." Many of these same people, while defending the neighborhood, also managed to transcend their isolationist stance and participate with their neighbors in Greenpoint and Williamsburg to find solutions to local problems. Previous chapters documented how whites and people of color worked together in planning and stood together in protest. Relationships developed to the point that residents supported their comrades' efforts by attending meetings and actions even when the outcome would not directly affect them. The excitement of victory and strategic planning was contagious. On an informal level, a number of friendships as well as romantic and political relationships formed cross racially, because of the Coalition experience. White women from Greenpoint and women of color from Williamsburg became friends. A white, Greenpoint woman was the main campaigner for an Hispanic woman of Williamsburg seeking public office. White community organizers assisted black community leaders, and black community organizers worked with white community organizations. An Hispanic woman from Williamsburg and a Polish man from Greenpoint were married. In some cases, people moved from one neighborhood to another. For example, some people left Greenpoint to live in Williamsburg, while others left Williamsburg for Greenpoint. The social networks which formed through the Coalition enabled people to obtain housing in each neighborhood. Alliances, between community organizations that focused on the delivery of services, such as summer jobs and year round training programs for youth, and the federal summer food program were also made across ethnic and racial lines. The Coalition provided the opportunity for the social exchanges described, and challenged people's stereotypical thinking about race and ethnicity. The opportunity to mix with people from different ethnic groups within the community may not have occurred without the existence and structure of the Coalition. In fact as discussed in an earlier chapter, some respondents recognize the continued need for a coalition to negotiate ethnic and racial divisions within Greenpoint-Williamsburg, and to advocate for integration. This acknowledgement on the part of former Coalition participants suggests a change in their political and race consciousness.

Through the Coalition's approach of leadership training and activism, members also developed class consciousness. That is to say, they reached a level of recognition regarding their class position. Each time their requests concerning community problems were ignored, they arrived at a better understanding of the dynamics of social class. Through the process of action, people recognized their collective deprivation. This point is demonstrated in Christine Noschese's film, Metropolitan Avenue, which documents women's activism in Greenpoint-Williamsburg. Most of those women filmed were leaders of the Coalition, and many of the events presented were Coalition actions. One woman interviewed in the film conveys her sense of class relations by stating,

> People were pitted against each other. The poor was pitted against the middle class. And the rich, they were on there by themselves in that little old corner of theirs. They made all the rules and we were the ones that, we had to suffer. And it's not so because the middle class and the poor is really the same in my estimation. And again, with a lot of things, with the closing of the fire department. The fire department was the one on the north side. They wanted to close that one. They said we had another one. Why shouldn't we, each community have our own...communities then would fight. And that's what happens, people fight with one another and what we should do is fight the ones who start the problems and that's the government and the City. Maybe that's where we should make the real big turn and say, "we pay the taxes,

> and this is what we want and we need in our community."
> And no one is gonna fight against the blacks, the Puerto
> Ricans, the whites, or anything like this. It's for everyone.

Residents learned first-hand that the community of Greenpoint-Williamsburg was not a priority for public policy because it was a low income area. The tradition of policy making in New York City has been to disregard poor communities, while maintaining affluent areas. This approach is based on the notion that low income people, unlike their more affluent counterparts, do not vote and are not organized. Through protest activities, the Greenpoint-Williamsburg community created an atmosphere of discomfort for policy makers, so they could not easily neglect the community's requests for action. The successes achieved by this method conveyed to the community that there is power in collective action.

As noted earlier, feminism was introduced to the community of Greenpoint-Williamsburg during the mid 1970's. Earlier chapters described the formation of the CETA consortium, which involved the creation of community organizations. Among those established was the National Congress of Neighborhood Women (NCNW). NCNW provided women of Greenpoint-Williamsburg with leadership training and a college program in the community. Many women involved in NCNW later became leaders of the Coalition. The outcome of NCNW's programs has been called "working class feminism" (Haywoode 1991). The combination of formal education through NCNW, and opportunities for women's participation in the Coalition, allowed for the development of feminist consciousness. As Noschese remarks in Metropolitan Avenue,

> ...These women who took leadership in their community to
> fight for things they believed in, and in the process... they
> developed an inner strength inside themselves. And they,
> regardless of whether they won or they lost, or what the issue
> was, it sort of changed their lives. Just the fact that they acted
> to fight for what they believed in. That is sort of what I guess
> power is about...But what they...decided was that something
> meant something to them...and they decided to work for it
> and work for other people, and it really changed them. It
> changed them like nothing in their lives had changed them
> before.

Furthermore, this study demonstrates that participants of the

Coalition were transformed by the experience. Many maintain the cross racial relationships and networks formed by their involvement in the Coalition. Moreover, many continued their community work after the Coalition's decline and took with them a different view of politics, government, and the workings of a democratic system, that developed from their activism. This is best illustrated by those Coalition leaders who are presently members of the community board. On the board, they view their role as one of "smoke screen," and "pawns," and continue to suggest protest as the mechanism to get the community served by the City. These leaders acquired skills from Coalition activities, such as public speaking and analyses of power, which served them as they carried on community work. Former Coalition participants are presently found in various local settings. Some people remained active in the community organization that they represented at the Coalition. Others have devoted themselves to resolving environmental hazards in Greenpoint-Williamsburg. Some residents who worked on planning the future of McCarren Park under the auspices of the Coalition, proceed in their efforts. Recently, a protest was held to hold government accountable for the adequate replacement of trees throughout the community scheduled for removal because of infestation by an Asian beetle. Additional Coalition leaders have entered local politics by being elected to public office, or to the school board, hired as a political aide, or appointed to the community board. They continue to be informed and shaped by their training from the Coalition.

Finally, this study raises questions regarding citizen participation. As a democratic society do we want ordinary people to partake in the process of generating their priorities on issues? Do we believe in the "dream"[1] and want people to develop positive relationships with others who are from different ethnic and racial groups? Or do we want to limit input by ordinary people to an electoral process and allow political and economic leaders to propose plans that are channeled through a formal process? This study suggests the ability of community organizations to confront contemporary urban problems such as disinvestment, poverty, the lack of affordable housing, drug abuse, racial tension, and crime. Through models like the Coalition, the frustration experienced by ordinary people could be focused to bring about changes in urban policy, while also building communities capable of accepting cultural variation. In the aftermath of race riots, the search for vehicles which empower ordinary people is crucial.

This analysis suggests that accomplishments are possible on a grass roots level when resources are available to communities. It indicates the need for community organizations to be fiscally self-sufficient instead of falling victim to the whims of government funding agencies and foundations. Resource dependency (Aldrich 1979) creates limits to citizen participation (Gittell 1980). In reviewing the Coalition's achievements it is apparent that private investment would be an enlightened venture. Residents and local institutions, including churches and businesses, benefit from neighborhood improvements. They are likely resources to be drawn upon to support the organizing efforts of community organizations.

The contemporary relevance of the Coalition and other organizing efforts which began in the 1970's is their evolution into models of organizations which are financially self sufficient, and view organizers as professionals. One example is the Industrial Areas Foundation (IAF), which is Saul Alinsky's legacy and a national network of neighborhood organizing projects. IAF has twenty-eight organizations in twenty cities across the United States (Perry 1990). All projects are staffed by organizers trained by IAF, and supported through membership dues, copying the union model, and grants from church congregations. By accepting no government funds these contemporary coalitions are more politically independent than earlier ones. They also spend little money on administration, and use the skills of their organizers and leaders for political action, rather than on fund raising and grant writing. These organizations have reached a level of political sophistication to have an impact on national,[2] state, and local electoral campaigns and public policy appointments.

This study of community mobilization and coalition building in northern Brooklyn arrives at a prototype for democratic action which more effectively empowers ordinary people from different races and ethnic groups, and allows for greater political participation than electoral politics. It is a model of citizen organizations run and funded by citizens. The old urban political machines could be replaced by citizens organizations whose agenda is not limited to voting, and who have the potential to ignite the creation of an urban agenda by activating a coalition of working class ethnics and minorities.

This examination of the GWCOCO offers a keyhole view into a community in which the traditional definition of political participation is broadened to include the struggle and mobilization of citizens on a local level to meet local needs. This study also indicates that expanding the definition of politics to include community activism adds women to leadership roles whereby, in contrast, electoral and union activities are dominated mostly by men. Furthermore, the activism and accomplishments of the Coalition presents a process more akin to workplace organizing than club house politics, which has been a focus of investigations of local politics. Yet as discussed earlier, an outcome of the Coalition experience is the politicization of people which can include a heightened interest in electoral politics. Thus, the process of community struggle can serve as a precursor to electoral activity and other forms of political behavior.

Those residents of Greenpoint-Williamsburg involved in the Coalition were empowered before the concept of empowerment became a political "buzz word" of the 1980's and 90's. The Coalition was based on principles of inclusion and pluralism, which promoted the occupancy of positions of leadership by women, people of color, and poor people, along with whites from varying ethnic backgrounds. This organizational structure resulted in a reassessment of people's stereotypes. The testament of empowerment associated with the process of struggle is the fact that ordinary people managed to upset their elected officials, New York City's urban planners and bureaucrats, to draw the print and electronic media, and to engage in successful negotiation with the Mayor of a city of nearly eight million people.

Social scientists frequently miss or minimize social groupings and activities on a local level that do not fit existing paradigms. Studies on elites, labor, and social movements are evaluated as analyses of political behavior. This study should be viewed as another attempt to contribute to a broader examination of political behavior. The GWCOCO currently has numerous contemporary descendants in cities across America. The significance and potential of these projects continue, for the most part, to be unrecognized by social scientists.

Notes

[1] I am referring to the use of the term dream used by Martin Luther King.
[2] Henry Cisneros, former Secretary of Housing and Urban Development (HUD) in the Clinton administration, comes out of an IAF organization.

METHODOLOGICAL NOTE

This study was carried out through the use of a variety of research methods. First, participant observation was employed. In 1979, I was elected to the Coalition's board of directors as an Area Vice President representing Central Williamsburg. There were three vice presidents elected from each sector of the community. I was viewed as a delegate from the Italian community. As a member of the board of directors, I had access to all Coalition meetings, the Coalition office, and organizing and support staff. Second, content analysis was used. I examined the following materials: newspaper accounts of Coalition events, progress reports sent by the Coalition's Executive Director to funding sources, grant proposals written by Coalition staff members and sent to funding sources, programs from the Coalition's annual conventions, and flyers which advertised Coalition meetings, local issues that the organization would undertake, and upcoming events. Finally, interviews were also utilized. During the summer of 1991, I contacted and interviewed 20 individuals who were Coalition leaders or organizers. These interviews were open ended and lasted between 1-2 hours each. In general, I asked each person to reflect on the Coalition and his/her experiences as a member of the organization, and to articulate current perceptions and thoughts about it. Most people welcomed the opportunity to discuss the Coalition, and viewed their involvement as a positive time in their lives in which they accomplished something. Most people enjoyed the interview. Their names have been deleted or changed.

REFERENCES

Abrahamson, Mark. 1996. Urban Enclaves: Identity and Place in America. New York: St. Martin's Press.

Ackelsberg, Martha A. 1988. Communities, Resistance, and Women's Activism: Some Implications for a Democratic Polity. In Women and the Politics of Empowerment, edited by Ann Bookman and Sandra Morgen. Philadelphia: Temple University Press.

Aldrich, Howard E. 1979. Organizations and Environments. Englewood Cliffs, New Jersey: Prentice-Hall Publishers.

Alinsky, Saul. 1971. Rules for Radicals. New York: Vintage Books.

Aronowitz, Stanley. 1983. Working Class Hero. New York: The Pilgrim Press.

Ayres Jr., B. Drummond. 1996. The Expanding Hispanic Vote Shakes Republican Strongholds. The New York Times, Sunday, November 10.

Barron, James. 1996. Sale of Grand Rabbi's Home Is Upheld. The New York Times, Wednesday, July 3.

Bernstein, Irving. 1970. The Lean Years: A History of the American Worker, 1920-1933. Baltimore: Penguin Books.

Bernstein, Irving. 1971. Turbulent Years: A History of the American Worker, 1933-1941. Boston: Houghton Mifflin Co.

Berube, Maurice R. and Marilyn Gittell. 1969. Confrontation at Ocean Hill-Brownsville. New York: Praeger Publishers.

Bookman, Ann and Sandra Morgen. 1988. Women and the Politics of Empowerment. Philadelphia: Temple University Press.

Boyte, Harry. 1980. The Backyard Revolution. Philadelphia: Temple University Press.

_____. 1984. Community Is Possible. New York: Harper & Row Publishers.

Brecher, Jeremy. 1972. Strike!. San Francisco: Straight Arrow Books.

Campbell, Angus and Phillip Converse, Warren E. Miller, Donald Stokes. 1960. The American Voter. New York: Wiley.

Castells, Manuel. 1983. The City and the Grassroots. Berkeley: University of California Press.

Chancer, Lynn. forthcoming. Provoking Assaults: High Profile Crime Causes in Contemporary America. Berkeley: University of California Press.

Clavel, Pierre. 1986. The Progressive City: Planning and Participation, 1969-1984. New Brunswick, New Jersey: Rutgers University 1969-1985. Press.

Clavel, Pierre. 1991. Harold Washington and the Neighborhoods: Progressive City Government in Chicago, 1983-1987. New Brunswick: Rutgers University Press.

Crenson, Matthew A. 1983. Neighborhood Politics. Cambridge, Massachusetts: Harvard University Press.

Dahl, Robert A. 1961. Who Governs. New Haven: Yale University Press.

_____. 1973. Governing the Giant Corporation. In Corporate Power in America. Edited by Ralph Nader and Mark J. Green. New York: Grossman.

Delk, James D. 1995. Fires and Furies: The L.A. Riots: What Really Happened. Palm Springs, California: ETC Publications.

DeMartini, Joseph R. 1983. Social Movement Participation: Political Socialization, Generational Consciousness, and Lasting Effects. Youth and Society 15: 195-223.

DeSena, Judith N. 1990. Protecting One's Turf: Social Strategies for Maintaining Urban Neighborhoods. Lanham, Maryland: University Press of America.

DeSena, Judith N. 1994. Women: The Gatekeepers of Urban Neighborhoods. Journal of Urban Affairs Volume 16, Number 3 (1994).

deTocqueville, Alexis. (1956). Democracy in America. Edited by Richard D. Heffner. New York: Mentor Books.

Domhoff, G. William. 1979. The Powers That Be. New York: Vintage Books.

Dye, Thomas R. 1976. Who's Running America? Englewood Cliffs, New Jersey: Prentice-Hall.

Echols, Alice. 1989. Daring to be Bad: Radical Feminism in America 1967-1975. Minneapolis: University of Minnesota Press.

Elkin, Stephen. 1987. City and Regime in the American Republic. Chicago: University of Chicago Press.

Fainstein, Norman I. and Susan S. Fainstein. 1974. Urban Political Movements. New Jersey: Prentice-Hall.

Fantasia, Rick. 1988. Cultures of Solidarity. Berkeley: University of California Press.

Fitch, Robert. 1993. The Assassination of New York. New York: Verso.

Freeman, Jo. 1975. The Politics of Women's Liberation. New York: David McKay.

Freudenberg, Nick and Sally Kohn. 1982. The Washington Heights Health Action Project: A New Role for Social Service Workers in Community Organizing. Catalyst 4: 7-23.

Gamson, William A. 1975. Strategy of Protest. Homeland, Illinois: Dorsey Press.

Gans, Herbert. 1962. The Urban Villagers. New York: The Free Press.

Gelb, Joyce and Marilyn Gittell. 1986. Seeking Equality: The Rloe of Activist Women in Cities. In The Egalitarian City, edited by Janet K. Boles. New York: Praeger Publishers.

Gibbs, Lois. 1982. Love Canal. Albany, New York: The State University of New York Press.

Gittell, Marilyn. 1980. Limits To Citizen Participation: The Decline of Community Organization. Beverly Hills, California: Sage Publications.

Gittell, Marilyn and Teresa Shtob. 1980. Changing Women's Roles in Political Volunteerism and Reform of the City. Signs: Journal of Women in Culture and Society 5: 64-75.

Goffman, Erving. 1959. The Presentation of Self in Everyday Life. New York: Doubleday Anchor Books.

Hardy-Fanta, Carol.1993. Discovering Latina Women in Boston Politics. Harvard Journal of Hispanic Policy 7: 5-25.

Harrigan, John J. 1993. Empty Dreams, Empty Pockets: Class and Biasin American Politics. New York: Macmillan Publishing Company.

Haywoode, Terry L. 1989. Working Class Women and Neighborhood Politics. In Contemporary Readings in Sociology, edited by Judith N. DeSena. Dubuque, Iowa: Kendall-Hunt Publishing Company.
_____. 1991. Working Class Feminism: Creating a Politics of Community Connection and Concern. Unpublished Doctoral Dissertation. Graduate School and University Center, City University of New York.

Hocking, Patricia M. and C.T. Husbands. 1976. Why Is There No Socialism in the United States? White Plains: M.E. Sharpe.

Hofrichter, Richard. 1993. Toxic Struggles. Philadelphia: New Society

Publishers.

Howell, Joseph T. 1973. Hard Living on Clay Street. New York: Anchor
  Books.

Hunter, Floyd. 1953. Community Power Structure. Chapel Hill:
  University of North Carolina Press.

Huizinga, Johan. 1972. America. New York: Harper & Row.

Hunter, Albert. 1974. Symbolic Communities. Chicago: University of
  Chicago Press.

Jackman, Mary and Robert Jackman. 1983. Class Awareness in the
  United States. Berkeley: University of California Press.

Jenkins, J.C. 1985. The Politics of Insurgency. New York: Columbia
  University Press.

Kaplan, Temma. 1982. Female Consciousness and Collective Action:
  The Case of Barcelona, 1910-1918. Signs: Journal of Women
  in Culture and Society 7: 513-738.

Katznelson, Ira. 1982. City Trenches: Urban Politics and the Patterning
  of Class in the United States. Chicago: University of
  Chicago Press.

Kibria, Nazli. 1990. Power, Patriarchy, and Gender Conflict in the
  Vietnamese Immigrant Community. Gender & Society 4: 9-24.

Klein, Ethel. 1984. Gender Politics. Cambridge, Massachusetts: Harvard
  University Press.

Kleppner, Paul. 1982. Who Voted? The Dynamics of Electoral Turnout,
  1870-1980. New York: Praeger Publishers.

Komarovsky, Mirra. 1967. Blue Collar Marriage. New York: Vintage
  Books.

Kornblum, William. 1974. Blue Collar Community. Chicago:

University of Chicago Press.

Kranzler, George. 1995. Hasidic Williamsburg: A Contemporary American Hasidic Community. Northvale, New Jersey:-Jason Aronson, Inc.

Krase, Jerome. 1979. "Stigmatized Places, Stigmatized People: Crown Heights and Prospect-Lefferts Gardens." In Brooklyn, U.S.A., edited by Rita Seiden Miller. New York: Brooklyn College Press.

Krauss, Celene. 1993. Blue Collar Women and Toxic Waste Protests: The Process of   Politicization. In Toxic Struggles, edited by Richard Hofrichter. Philadelphia: New Society Publishers.

Krauss, Celene. 1989. Community Struggles and the Shaping of Democratic Consciousness. Sociological Forum 4: 227-239.

Lawson, Ronald and Stephen E Barton. 1980. Sex Roles in Social Movements: A Case Study of the Tenant Movement in New York City. Signs: Journal of Women in Culture and Society 6: 230-247.

Lea, James F. 1982. Political Consciousness and American Democracy. Jackson, Mississippi: University Press of Mississippi.

Lichten, Eric. 1986. Class, Power, and Austerity: The New York City Fiscal Crisis. South Hadley, Massachusetts: Bergin and Garvey.

Liebow, Elliot. 1967. Tally's Corner. Boston: Little, Brown and Company.

Lofland, Lynn. 1975. The "Thereness" of Women. In Another Voice, edited by Marcia Millman and Rosabeth Moss Kanter. New York: Anchor Books.

Logan, John R. and Harvey Molotch. 1987. Urban Fortunes. Berkeley: University of California Press.

Luttrell, Wendy. 1988. The Edison School Struggle: The Reshaping of

Working Class Education and Women's Consciousness. In Women and the Politics of Empowerment, edited by Ann Bookman and Sandra Morgen. Philadelphia: Temple University Press.

Lynd, Robert and Helen Lynd. 1929. Middletown. New York: Harcourt, Brace.

McAdam, D. 1982. Political Process and the Development of Black Insurgency 1930-1970. Chicago: University of Chicago Press.

McCourt, Kathleen. 1977. Working Class Women and Grass Roots Politics. Bloomington: Indiana University Press.

Mills, C. Wright. 1956. The Power Elite. New York: Oxford University Press.

Mollenkopf, John Hull. 1992. A Phoenix in the Ashes: The Rise and Fall of the Koch Coalition. Princeton, New Jersey: Princeton University Press.

Monti, Daniel. 1990. Race, Redevelopment and the New Company Town. Albany,   New York: State University of New York Press.

Moore, Kelly. 1994. The Development of New Channels of Political Access. Paper presented at the annual meeting of the American Sociological Association, August 8, Los Angeles.

Morgen, Sandra. 1988. It's the Whole Power of the City Against Us!: The Development of Political Consciousness in a Women's Health Care Coalition. In Women and the Politics of Empowerment, edited by Ann Bookman and Sandra Morgen. Philadelphia: Temple University Press.

Morris, Aldon D. 1984. The Origins of the Civil Rights Movement. New York: The Free Press.

Morris, Aldon D. 1992. Political Consciousness and Collective Action. In Frontiers in Social Movement Theory. Edited by Aldon D. Morris and Carol McClung Mueller. New Haven: Yale

University Press.

Nagourney, Adam 1996. "One Convention Goal: Displaying Party's Advantage with   Women". The New York Times, August 29, A1.

Naples, Nancy A. 1998. Grassroots Warriors: Activist Mothering, Community Work, and the War on Poverty. New York: Routledge.

_____. 1991. Just What Needed To Be Done: The Political Practice of Women Community Workers in Low-Income Neighborhoods. Gender & Society 5: 478-494.

_____. 1992. Activist Mothering: Cross-Generational Continuity in the Community Work of Women from Low-Income Urban Neighborhoods. Gender & Society 6: 441-463

Nardulli, Peter F., Jon K. Dalager, and Donald E. Greco. 1996. Voter Turnout in U.S. Presidential Elections. PS: Political Science and Politics. September.

New York City Planning Commission. 1969. Plan for New York City: A Proposal. Part 3, Brooklyn.

Nie, Norman, Sidney Verba, and John Petrocik. 1976. The Changing American Voter. Cambridge: Harvard University Press.

Noschese, Christine. 1991. Metropolitan Avenue. New Day Films.

Oberschall, A. 1973. Social Conflicts and Social Movements. Englewood Cliffs, New Jersey: Prentice-Hall.

_____. 1978. The Decline of the 1960's Social Movements. In Research in Social Movements I, edited by L. Kriesberg. Greenwich, Connecticut: JAI Press.

Olson, M. 1965. The Logic of Collective Action: Public Goods and the Theory of Groups. Cambridge, Massachusetts: Harvard University Press.

Pardo, Mary. 1990. Mexican American Women Grassroots Community
    Activists: "Mothers of East Los Angeles." Frontiers: A Journal
    of Women Studies 11: 1-7.

Perry, Cynthia. 1990. IAF 50 Years: Organizing For Change. Industrial
    Areas Foundation.

Pichardo, Nelson. 1988. Resource Mobilization: An Analysis of
    Conflicting Theoretical Variations. Sociological Quarterly 29:
    97-110.

Piven, Frances Fox and Richard A. Cloward. 1977. Poor People's
    Movements. New York: Pantheon Books.

Rainwater, Lee, Richard P. Coleman, and Gerald Handel. 1959.
    Workingman's Wife. New York: Oceana Publications.

Rieder, Jonathan. 1985. Canarsie. Cambridge, Massachusetts: Harvard
    University Press.

Ross, Timothy. 1995. Quantifying the Impact of Industrial Areas
    Foundation Community Organizing on Local Housing Markets
    in New York City: A Comparative Study of 59 Community
    Districts. Paper presented at the annual meeting of the New
    York State Political Science Association, April 28-29, New
    York City.

Rubin, Lillian Breslow. 1976. Worlds of Pain. New York: Basic Books.

Salak, John. 1993. The Los Angeles Riots: America's Cities in Crisis.
    Brookfield, Connecticut: Millbrook Press.

Schattschneider, E.E. 1960. The Semi-Sovereign People. New York:
    Holt, Rinehart and Winston.

Schmitt, Eric. 1996. Half the Electorate, Perhaps Satisfied or Bored, Sat
    Out Voting. New York Times, Thursday, November 7.

Schoenberg, Sandra. 1981. Some Trends in the Community Participation
    of Women in Their Neighborhoods. In Women and the
    American City, edited by Catharine R. Stimpson, Elsa Dixler,
    Martha J. Nelson, and Kathryn B. Yatrakis. Chicago: University

of Chicago Press.

Schoenberg, Sandra and Irene Dabrowski. 1978. Factors Which Enhance
the Participation of Women in Neighborhood Social Life. Paper
presented at the annual meeting of the American Sociological
Association. September 5-8.

Seifer, Nancy. 1976. Nobody Speaks For Me! New York: Simon and
Schuster.

Shienbaum, Kim Ezra. 1984. Beyond the Electoral Connection.
Philadelphia: University of Pennsylvania Press.

Sites, William. 1994. Urban Regime Theory and Pressure: New York's
Development Policy Since 1975. Paper presented at the annual
meeting of the   Eastern   Sociological   Society,   March 17-20,
Baltimore.

Squire, Peverill, James Lindsay, Cary Covington, and Eric Smith. 1995.
Dynamics of Democracy. Madison, Wisconsin: Brown and
Benchmark.

Stack, Carol. 1974. All Our Kin. New York: Harper and Row.

Susser, Ida. 1982. Norman Street. New York: Oxford University Press.

_____. 1988. Working Class Women, Social Protest, and Changing
Ideologies. In Women and the Politics of Empowerment, edited by
Ann Bookman and Sandra Morgan. Philadelphia: Temple
University Press.

Suttles, Gerald. 1968. The Social Order of the Slum. Chicago: University
of Chicago Press.

Tannen, Deborah. 1990. You Just Don't Understand. New York:
Ballantine Books.

Teixeira, Roy A. 1992. The Disappearing American Voter. Washington,
D.C.: The Brookings Institution.

Tilly, Charles. 1978. From Mobilization to Revolution. Reading,
Massachusetts: Addison-Wesley.

Toner, Robin. 1996. With G.O.P Congress the Issue, 'Gender Gap' Is Growing Wider. The New York Times, April 21, A1.

Ui, Shiori. 1991. "Unlikely Heroes": The Evolution of Female Leadership in a   Cambodian Ethnic Enclave. In Ethnography Unbound, edited by Michael Burawoy et. al. Berkeley: University of California Press.

U.S. Bureau of the Census. 1990 Census of Population and Housing, Summary Tape File 3A.

Vanneman, Reeve and Lynn Cannon. 1987. The American Perception of Class. Philadelphia: Temple University Press.

Verba, Sidney and Norman H. Nie. 1972. Participation in America: Political Democracy and Social Equality. New York: Harper and Row Publishers.

Vidich, Arthur J. and Joseph Bensman. 1968. Small Town in Mass Society. Princeton: Princeton University Press.

Weber, Max. 1947. The Theory of Social and Economic Organization. New York: The Free Press.

West, Guida and Lois Rhoda Blumberg.   1990.   Women and Social Protest. New York: Oxford University Press.

Whyte, William F. 1955. Street Corner Society. Chicago: University of Chicago Press.

Williams, Terry and William Kornblum. 1985. Growing Up Poor. Lexington, Massachusetts: D.C. Heath and Company.

Wolfinger, Raymond and Stephen J. Rosenstone. 1980. Who Votes. New Haven: Yale University Press.

Wright, Erik Olin. 1985. Classes. London: Verso.

INDEX

ABOUT THE AUTHOR

Judith N. DeSena is an Associate Professor of Sociology at St. John's University in New York City. Her research interests focus on working class neighborhoods, race and ethnic relations among locals, and women's community activism. Dr. DeSena has lived and worked in working class neighborhoods throughout her life. Her work has drawn attention to the role of neighborhood women in maintaining and preserving their local culture and improving neighborhood conditions.

Dr. DeSena is author of Protecting One's Turf: Social Strategies for Maintaining Urban Neighborhoods (University Press of America, 1990), editor of an anthology entitled, Contemporary Readings in Sociology, (Kendall-Hunt Publishing Company, 1989) and co-editor with Jerome Krase of Italian Americans in a Multicultural Society (Forum Italicum, 1994). She has also published various articles in the area of residential segregation and gendered space.

Dr. DeSena's present study focuses on the community activism of women gentrifiers and their attempts to change local institutions and community power relations.